THE
SECRET
HEART

Joyce—

May the Lord bless you as
you embrace your secret heart.

This book is typeset in EB Garamond
Designed by Hannah Gaskamp

THE
SECRET
HEART

From Hiding to Wholeness
Through God's Delight in the Real You

OSCAR HASELDEN

"Behold, you delight in truth in the inward being, and you teach me wisdom in the secret heart."

PSALM 51:6 ESV

CONTENTS

CONTENTS

PREFACE

I never intended to write a book in the year 2020. Then again, I never intended to write a book in the years before or after 2020, either. While it's true that I majored in English, I did so because I found the major interesting and easy, not because I wanted to be a writer.

I originally planned for the section titled "The H.E.A.R.T. List" to be the entire book. I envisioned it as a severely brief guide people could use to access their thoughts and feelings. But I found I couldn't write "The H.E.A.R.T. List" without including at least some of my personal history, and including even some of my personal history ruined my desired goal of brevity.

On the afternoon of Sunday, May 24, 2020, I walked defeatedly into our kitchen and told my wife Elizabeth that "The H.E.A.R.T. List" felt like it was a sequel or at least part of a larger work. I also made myself admit a reality I didn't want to admit: that I had no idea how to move forward. I went to bed that evening feeling sad and mourning the loss of my very first writing project, which was barely a month old.

When my alarm sounded at 5:00 the next morning, Monday, May 25, 2020, I strongly considered hitting the snooze button and crawling back into bed. But I thought better of it and got in the shower. In the shower, I opened my YouVersion Bible app, pressed "Plans," pressed "M'Cheyne One Year Reading Plan," pressed "20 Missed Days"—because I was twenty days behind—pressed "May 4 Day 127," and listened as the narrator began the four readings included in Day 127: Numbers 15, Psalm 51, Isaiah 5, and Hebrews 12.

I stood in the shower and tried to follow along with the narrator, but the struggle was real. On top of my brain's early morning fog, I was also battling the lingering sadness of having given up on my book the day before. I found myself growing sleepier and sadder by the minute until the narrator said the phrase "the secret heart."

Something about the phrase jolted me awake and yanked me to attention. The phrase mesmerized and bewildered me. I began wondering if I'd heard what I thought I'd heard. After all, I had been through this exact one-year reading plan four or five times, yet I couldn't remember ever hearing the phrase "the secret heart." Was it even real? Or was my mind playing tricks on me? I didn't know, and I was determined to find out.

After completing "Day 127," I decided to go back through each of the four readings in search of the phrase "the secret heart." Starting with Numbers 15, I slowly scanned each verse but didn't find it, so I moved on to Psalm 51. Again, I scrolled down slowly, carefully reading each verse until I got to verse six. And there it was, "the secret heart."

Hey, hey! The phrase *was* real; I hadn't imagined it! Excited, I wanted to learn the fuller context of the verse, so I re-read verse six in its entirety. It read, "Behold, you delight in truth in the inward being, and you teach me wisdom in the secret heart."

The verse astonished me. Eighteen words precisely captured what I'd experienced with God over the previous eight years. The verse was the perfect summation of God's bringing me from hiding to wholeness while teaching me wisdom along the way. Now I *had* to know more, so I decided to read all of Psalm 51.

My heart pounded as I scrolled back to the top of the fifty-first psalm, and I nearly dropped my phone altogether when I saw the note introducing the chapter: "To the choirmaster. A Psalm of David, when Nathan the prophet went to him, after he had gone in to Bathsheba."

After reading the note, the hair on my arms and the back of my neck stood straight up. Knowing that David's adulterous affair with Bathsheba was the context of Psalm 51 in general, and verse six in particular, made the moment feel all the more divine. I instantly realized that Psalm 51:6 was the inspiration I needed to tell my story and the outline of the book I was meant to write. I also knew the title for my book would be *The Secret Heart*.

Writing *The Secret Heart* has been one of the most rewarding experiences of my life. It's also been challenging and painful at times. But whatever pains I've suffered while writing this book pale in comparison to how painful it would've been for me to *not* write it. Overall, writing *The Secret Heart* has brought me great joy.

But writing *The Secret Heart* was not without its fair share of difficulties, though the difficulties had nothing to do with summoning the energy required to organize the many, disparate thoughts into a comprehensive and cohesive story. The great difficulty in writing *The Secret Heart* was this: How does a person faithfully describe their encounters with the Almighty?

Human words are great, but not great enough to capture the fullness of God nor His interactions with His people. In the book,

I describe sensing God's Presence, hearing His words and answering His questions, seeing fire and ferocity on His face and in His eyes, and encountering His radiant joy. These descriptions are my best attempt at capturing the uncapturable.

While I write in places that "God said," or "He spoke," I didn't hear an actual, audible voice like I do when Elizabeth or any other person speaks to me. It's more like His words pop up somewhere within me sometime during our interaction, and it's easiest to describe it as His speaking. The reason I've used phrases such as "God said," is because the result is the same as it is when a person speaks to me.

For example, Elizabeth's communications to and with me produce a series of thoughts, feelings, and memories from which I grow, change, and respond. And although it was more like God would deposit an idea, question, thought, Bible verse, or a word like "welcome" within me, whatever He deposited would produce a series of thoughts, feelings, and memories by which I was made different.

I'd like to offer readers an exercise that may bring clarity as to *how* I experienced these interactions with God.

Close your eyes and call to mind a parent, or spouse, or a sibling. It can be anyone; go with whomever most readily comes to mind.

Now imagine that person looks at you and says, "I love you." If I asked whether you saw a person in your mind, I bet you'd say you did. But if I asked whether it felt the same as seeing a live person standing in front of or next to you, I bet you'd say it didn't.

Furthermore, if I asked whether the person you called to mind spoke to you, I bet you'd say they did. But if I asked whether you *heard* their words, I bet you'd say that you "sort of" heard them. You didn't *exactly* hear them, or at least not like the way you'd hear me if we were talking over a cup of coffee—my treat, of course!

What you experienced is *somewhat* like hearing a person's words. But it's also somewhat like thinking the words and even a little bit like feeling the words too.

I admit that the above exercise generates, at best, a poor and shabby comparison to the encounters with God as I've described in *The Secret Heart*. But it will have served its purpose if it helps you understand the nuance embedded in my descriptions of when I "saw" God and when God "said" this or that to me.

There's just no way to completely capture exactly what my encounters with God were like. But I assure you the experiences were very real and very wonderful and that what I've written is exactly what I perceived. Nothing has been embellished or sensationalized.

Finally, as you prepare to read *The Secret Heart*, I want to make a few critical acknowledgments:

I believe the Bible is the inspired Word of God. The Bible is inerrant and infallible; my book is not. God's Word is authoritative; my word is not.

I don't intend for anyone to consider my book as on par with the Bible, because it's not. What *I* say about God cannot take precedence over what God has already said about Himself in His word.

Furthermore, my encounters with God, as well as the words I've used to describe both God and those encounters, should agree with the rest of the Bible. If any part of my experience or any of my words used to describe God or said experience is found to conflict with any part of the Bible, then my experience and my words are to be dismissed as wrong and unacceptable.

The Secret Heart is not prescriptive. I am not guaranteeing that if you do exactly what I did you'll get exactly what I got. Actually, I can guarantee that your experience will *not* be identical to mine, because God will lead and guide you according to *your* specific needs and according to His good pleasure.

The only guarantees I can and will ever make are those that are in keeping with His timeless and unchanging nature. For example, I can guarantee God will delight in truth in your inward being, not because *I* experienced His delight when I was honest before Him, but because God *said* He delights in truth in the inward being (Psalm 51:6). I can guarantee that God will serve you, because Jesus said He is among us as one who serves and that He and His Father—God—are one (Luke 22:27; John 10:30).

I hope you'll read *The Secret Heart* through the lens Paul gave us in 1 Thessalonians 5:20-21: "Do not despise prophecies, but test everything; hold fast what is good." And I hope *The Secret Heart* encourages a greater willingness in you to be honest before God and to admit your shame, and that you also experience His delight as you offer Him the truths of your inward being.

THE
SECRET
HEART

INTRODUCTION

I have a secret heart, and so do you. The secret heart stores what's truest about us. It's where you'll find the real you. It's where I found the real me.

I have a secret fear, and so do you. I'm afraid that parts of the real me are unacceptable. I'm afraid those unacceptable parts will keep me from enjoying the relationships, the connections, and the sense of belonging I so desperately crave.

I try hard to hide those parts, and I bet you do too. You and I hide the parts of ourselves we're afraid won't get a Like, a Retweet, or a Share. And we market the parts that will.

I wrote *The Secret Heart* for those who hide, because hiding the real you is hard and deeply painful. This book is for those who hide and use alcohol, drugs, or sex to numb their inevitable pain. But it's also for those who numb their pain with fatherhood and motherhood, or religious legalism, or money, or social activism. I wrote *The Secret Heart* for those who hide—*however* you may hide—because I want you to know that you are not alone.

In the following pages, you'll learn why and how I hid the real me. You'll see how God encouraged me out from hiding and then looked upon the real me with radiant joy. You'll discover some of the wisdom God granted me along the way, and you'll get a practical example of how I connect with and process what's going on in my secret heart.

I hope my story is the encouragement you need to explore why and how you may be hiding, and the inspiration you need to embrace the real you. May God shine His radiant joy upon you and teach you wisdom in your secret heart.

PART ONE

THE BEGINDING

ONE

GAME OF TAG

In the 1950s, my parents gave a religious cult nearly complete control of their lives. The cult warned that the world had been damned to hell and that only the cult's leader knew how to escape God's coming wrath. My parents unplugged from most of society—as ordered by their leader—but their involvement in the cult made them feel disillusioned, remorseful, and ashamed.

My parents responded to these feelings in radically different ways. My dad became almost totally withdrawn. He distrusted everyone, especially himself. He spoke only when he had to, and even then with great reluctance as if the act of speaking aloud could result in death. My dad felt ashamed for letting the cult control him, and this shame became his enduring legacy. His failure to protect himself and his family from the cult was a stain he could not blot out or forgive.

My mom took a different tack; she expanded outwardly. She started taking piano lessons, enrolled herself in college courses on music theory, and dreamed of one day teaching piano to others. My mom also began longing to have another child—a longing she insisted came from God—despite already having a twenty-two-year-old son and an eighteen-year-old daughter. I was that child.

I was born on June 17, 1977. I was born at home because my parent's cult leader said it was a sin for my mom to see a doctor or go to a hospital. My mom, who was forty-four years old, gave birth to me naturally in the morning and by that evening was up fixing dinner for her family.

By the time I was born, my parents had spent nearly thirty years in their oppressive cult, though their time in the cult would eventually come to an end. When my dad announced to the cult that he was retiring from his company, the cult leader said dad was too young and needed to keep working and, one would presume, tithing. But when Dad tried to unretire, he learned that his position had already been filled. To keep working, Dad would have to accept a transfer to the company's central office in Columbia, South Carolina, and that's exactly what he did.

We moved to Columbia when I was seven years old. And while my parents used the physical distance to gradually pull away and then break free from the cult, they were unable to distance themselves from the traumas they'd already suffered. This trauma had rendered my parents as unfit for thriving in the world as I was, and this shared unfitness—more than love—was our primary bond.

While my childhood was free of physical violence and my basic needs were always met, my more complex—and perhaps greater— needs went unmet. My parents couldn't move beyond their painful past, and their obsession with it consumed the attention, competency, and compassion I needed to feel protected, nurtured, developed, guided, and loved.

My parents—especially my dad—were stuck in the past and were therefore unable to make me feel welcomed. And not being welcomed by my parents made me feel alone in the present and terrified of the future.

I was terrified of the future because it looked like a giant, scary, undefined monster with endless ways to get me. I lived in constant fear of meeting new people or having new experiences, because they threatened to expose just how unprotected and unprepared I was. This constant fear made my life feel like a game of tag where everything could be "it," but nothing could be "base."

For example, the last days of class during elementary school were normally festive occasions, but for me, they were dreaded days filled with lament. While my classmates were busy anticipating the joys of summer, I was busy worrying about how the next grade might expose my parents' incompetence. I feared that if people learned my parents were incompetent, they'd have me forcibly removed from my home and put into a home for neglected and abused children.

Also, I hated seeing the reflexive, automatic fear in people's eyes when they met my dad and learned his age; he was fifty-three years old with a head full of white hair when I was born. Their fear *for* me became fear *in* me and made me wonder if I should be worried that dad might suddenly die. When Dad took a nap, I would watch his chest and, like an anxious parent, feel relieved to see that he was still breathing.

I despised this parent-child role reversal, and I despised living in fear. But the worst part was knowing that no matter how much I wished my life could be different, my parent's inadequacies would make sure it stayed the same.

I resented my parents for having a child when it was clear—at least to me—they weren't ready to nurture a child or to meet a child's deepest needs. My resentment toward my parents eventually turned into feeling embarrassed that I was their child. Feeling embarrassed over my parents made me ashamed of myself, and this shame became the belief that I was unacceptable.

I wanted to be accepted, and I wanted to belong. But I worried that the affiliation with my parents would be a stench I couldn't wash off and that would follow me wherever I'd go. My parents weren't going to change, and I couldn't swap families, so I began to dream of a future without my parents.

TWO

"THE BIG O"

I declared my parents dead to me in the fifth grade. It was the hardest and most painful decision of my life to that point. I loved my dad and mom—or at least I *wanted* to—but I felt there was no way I could remain connected to them *and* be accepted. I feared I would never be welcomed and accepted by others if they thought my parents and I were a packaged deal.

During this part of my childhood, I liked to imagine that I'd been taken in by a wealthy, cultured, and cool family, the kind of family I saw in movies and on television. The family would instill in me the beliefs, the behaviors, and the style associated with people who were accepted and belonged. Then I would return to my school, and my friends would be flabbergasted by my transformation. I would finally be accepted and welcomed, and everyone would want to be my friend.

Unfortunately, however, those sweet imaginings never materialized, and I was left in the same house, with the same parents, and I remained untransformed.

By the sixth grade, I was fed up with feeling ashamed, and I decided I'd either turn myself into the person others would accept or die trying. But it would be hard, if not impossible, to find that acceptance during my middle school years, because while everyone else was going through pubescent changes, I stayed the same—glaringly undersized.

All my life I had *felt* different than everyone else, but I was now starting to *look* different than everyone else too. My height and weight hadn't been a big deal when everyone was cute and little, but as more and more of my friends were turning into gangly adolescents, I started to feel ashamed of my small size.

I became desperate to grow. At home, I would pour tall glasses of Coburg Vitamin D Whole Milk hoping God would use the milk to make me grow like a priest hopes the communion wine will be used to make him holy. But my desperate hopes were deferred, and I entered high school standing under five feet tall and weighing less than a hundred pounds.

My stature earned me the nickname "The Big O," precisely because there was nothing big about me. I didn't hate the nickname, just the irony behind it. No one, not even my closest friends, could understand how my body's diminutive size and lack of development tortured me.

For example, when my buddies and I would listen to music, they would often ask me to sing the high notes they no longer could, since their voices had deepened and mine had not. They would laugh in amazement when I hit those notes, and while I was thankful to be included in the group, I felt more like their freak than their friend.

I despised feeling like a freak, and nothing made me feel like a freak more than girls, relationships, and talking about sex. My buddies were obsessed with girls; since I hadn't gone through puberty, I honestly didn't see what all the fuss was about. My buddies loved to talk about sex and to brag about what they had done and with whom they had done it. I was too embarrassed and ashamed to admit that I hadn't done anything with anyone, so I began to hide my real self in lies.

I lied and said that I had made out with girls, instead of admitting that I never had, that I didn't know how, and that even if I did, high school girls weren't interested in making out with a boy who could pass for being in elementary school. I lied and said that I looked forward to having sex, instead of admitting that I was terrified by the thought of it, instead of confessing I was afraid of a girl seeing my prepubescent penis, instead of revealing my shame of being the only kid I knew who was uncircumcised.

I would lie and say that I too viewed girls as sex objects and that I agreed girls served little purpose besides being the way that *us "men"* could have fun and explore our sexuality. Then I would look around at the faces of my buddies hoping to see that they approved of me, believed my lies, and didn't see how I truly felt: that sex scared me and was something that I absolutely was not ready to explore.

I finally hit puberty between the tenth and eleventh grades, growing taller by almost nine inches in less than two years. And as my body grew, so did my appetites for weed and women. I smoked a lot of pot and started looking at pornography, and I discovered the new sensation of lusting after women.

I learned how to use lust to bypass my long-held fears of being physically inadequate. But I failed to realize that the small, short-term gains lust gave me were offset by the large, long-term costs I paid. Lust left me more ashamed of being honest and more afraid of being known in every area of my life, sex included.

I felt ashamed of being honest and afraid of being known because I feared being rejected, and these feelings and fears were nothing new. But a subtle, almost invisible, shift had taken place; I could no longer blame my parents or my diminutive size as the reasons I feared being rejected. I now blamed myself.

Silently, and without my awareness or permission, the fear of being rejected had become a part of me, functioning like marrow in my bones. This marrow warehoused my stem cells, which turned into blood cells, which transported the fear of being known and rejected throughout my body and soul.

THREE

RE-SEARCHING

My twelfth-grade year was memorable, but not in a good way. I was expelled from high school just three months and two classes shy of graduation after having been written up too many times for disobedience and disrespect. I enrolled in a nearby adult education program to finish the government and economics courses I needed to earn my diploma.

My drug use escalated during this period, especially since I was now in school for just two hours per day. One weeknight, I met a long-time friend at the Burger King near our houses, and we planned to score some weed and get high. I sat in his car while he made some phone calls, and while sitting there, I noticed a man, apparently homeless, who was on his knees, then got up, only to get back on his knees again. I wanted to know what he was doing, so I got out of the car and asked. The man said he was a Messianic

Jew and that he was thanking God for the blessing of being hired to sweep the Burger King parking lot. My question answered, I got back in the car and waited on my friend.

My friend eventually found a girl who was willing to sell us some weed, and he and I drove separately to her house. The three of us got high and then watched some television. I started having a bad reaction to the drugs, and my heart began beating faster and faster. I grew increasingly worried, so I told my buddy and the girl what was happening. They assured me that I'd be fine, but I was unconvinced.

I decided I wanted to get medical help and drove myself to the nearby emergency room. I was admitted and given something to help calm me down. I was released well after midnight, went home, and went to sleep. When I woke up the next morning, I went out to my car, opened the glove box, grabbed my share of the weed, and flushed it down the toilet. My pot-smoking days were over.

My life had been built around getting high, and my friendships were based upon a shared dislike of being sober. Now that I *was* sober, I felt emboldened to live my life a little differently than I had before. I had a newfound ability to make different and better choices, even when I found myself in the same old situations or hanging out with the same old friends.

One such situation occurred when I went to a keg party in Newberry, South Carolina, with my long-time best friend, Travis. Travis had always loved beer and hated how pot made him feel; I had been the exact opposite. He and I went to the keg party, and I was the designated driver. Travis drank, I met new people, and we both had a good time. We left the party after midnight and made the forty-five-minute drive back to Columbia. We were both hungry, so we stopped at a Waffle House to get some breakfast.

The Waffle House in West Columbia sat adjacent to the Burger King. After Travis and I had gone inside, sat down, and ordered our meals, I casually scanned the diner and was shocked to see the same Messianic Jewish man I had previously met in the parking lot weeks before. He was sitting alone in the booth closest to the restrooms, and I told Travis that he had to meet this bizarre man. Travis and I walked over to the man's booth. I referenced when the man and I had previously met and asked if we could join him. He said yes.

The bizarre man's name was David. David opened his tattered Bible, flipped to the Book of Revelation, and began to share wild theories about the Rapture based upon his understanding of numerology and his knowledge of the Egyptian Pyramids. And he frequently referenced "Jesus, the one and only true Messiah of Israel." For some strange reason, I found all this riveting. I didn't even believe what the man had to say, but I found it spellbinding nonetheless.

When Travis and I finished our meals and went to leave, David followed us outside. He told me that Jesus Christ—the one and only true Messiah of Israel—was able and willing to forgive me of my sins. David asked if I wanted such forgiveness, and I contemplated the offer.

On the one hand, I wasn't sure that God, Jesus, Heaven, and Hell were even real. But if they were, and if sin existed, then I was certainly a sinner. Plus it was free, and I wouldn't be any worse off for having prayed a prayer.

"Why not?" I thought to myself. Then I recited the Sinner's Prayer, repeating the words of a homeless, Messianic Jewish man named David while standing in a Waffle House parking lot in the middle of the night.

Over several months, I had quit doing drugs, registered to be an organ donor should I die in a car crash, registered to vote should my vote ever be needed, and registered to have my sins forgiven should there be a God. I looked at each of these four decisions as positive and healthy choices, ranked in order of how much good I thought they could do for me and others.

Making choices that I could be proud of—choices that were almost universally accepted and applauded by others—was a new experience for me and one that I liked very much. I still felt tremendous shame over my past, and I certainly wasn't ready to let the world know my feelings, thoughts, dreams, and fears. But I was far more comfortable with people knowing this newest version of me than I had ever been with them knowing the old one.

This new version of me received his high school diploma via the adult education program; met, dated, and got his heart broken by a beautiful, young girl named Elizabeth; and got an Associate of Arts and Bachelor's in English from two colleges in Spartanburg, South Carolina.

I'd planned throughout college to become a high school English teacher, but I felt a very specific call to enter the ministry during the summer before my final semester.

After graduation, I was hired to be the youth minister at a church in Myrtle Beach, South Carolina. I worked at Myrtle Beach Community Church for three-and-a-half years, and the years were filled with things good and hard. The good included reconnecting with, and marrying, the girl named Elizabeth who had first broken my heart, while the hard parts of my life came mostly from my feeling inadequate at work as a youth minister.

Feeling inadequate drove me to continually ask God for wisdom in how to best lead the youth. For over two years, I asked God to give me a vision or plan for how my strengths could best be used to serve the youths' needs. And one day, He did.

The specifics of the plan aren't important, except to say that where the church was able to organize people to lead programs that impacted lives in the community, I felt I had to leverage relationships. I was disorganized and lacked any gifts of administration, so overseeing a bunch of programs was never going to work for me. My vision for the youth ministry became, almost out of necessity, one where I would teach people to reach people.

I felt equally relieved and excited to finally have a vision and plan I believed in, but the church elders and leadership didn't share my relief or excitement. Instead, I was summoned to a meeting with the church's executive pastor, who pulled out a copy of the youth ministry vision and the strategy I had written and previously submitted to him. He read the document and asked if it still accurately reflected my vision for the youth ministry. When I said that it did, he replied, "Well, we're going to have to let you go."

I was stunned.

"Wait, are you firing me?" I asked bewilderedly.

The executive pastor calmly replied, "Well, if you think it'd look better on your resume, we can say you resigned."

I was shocked, utterly devastated, and heartbroken. I felt God had given me a vision, an idea for moving forward into the future while considering my specific, personal strengths. In sharing that vision with the church's leaders, I was offering them a most intimate piece of my heart and soul, and I felt they had rejected both. I felt they had rejected *me*.

The church gave me a forty-five-day severance package. I had forty-five days to decide what I wanted to do with the rest of my life and where I wanted to do it. Worse, the decisions had to be made at a time when I felt maximally unsure of who I was, unclear of what I wanted, and unconfident in my strengths and abilities.

Not since childhood had I felt so vulnerable, powerless, and ashamed, and I hated those feelings as much at age twenty-six as I had then. I was desperate to be relieved of those feelings, so I ran in the opposite direction of the people, the places, and the profession that had hurt me so deeply. I ran and hid emotionally, relationally, and spiritually. I ran from God, and I ran from His people. I ran from Elizabeth, and I ran from myself.

I ran by resuming the search for the acceptable me—the search I had started in the sixth grade but had paused after becoming a Christian just before my eighteenth birthday—and I began to imagine myself becoming a person that was so successful and desirable that I'd be immune from rejection's bitter sting.

FOUR

FANCIFUL CURES

I ran and searched for the acceptable me, but at some point in the search, chasing the man I *wasn't* got interwoven with fleeing the man I was. The man I was had been fired abruptly and felt vulnerable, powerless, unacceptable, and ashamed. I wanted to figure out how to be a man that felt invincible, strong, accepted, and proud.

I reasoned that if work failures had been responsible for the unwanted feelings, then work success should produce the feelings I wanted. I pursued professional greatness in sales of cars, clothing, cell phones, and hydraulic valves. I worked in restaurants, first as a manager with aspirations of one day being the owner and later as a server in fine dining. I dreamed of becoming a successful real estate investor and venture capitalist, endeavors I funded by taking out a second mortgage on our home during the height of a real estate bubble.

Elizabeth was as supportive as she could be during my fruitless pursuit of professional greatness, but withholding my real self from her added stress to an already weak marriage. Our marriage was weak because neither of us knew ourselves very well, and the little bit of ourselves we *did* know made us feel uncomfortable.

One of the little uncomfortable bits we knew was that the way I naturally expressed love was not the way Elizabeth naturally received love, and vice versa, so that we both felt unloved. I was convinced that my feeling unloved meant Elizabeth didn't love me, and I let it be known that I no longer loved her some time between our fourth and fifth anniversaries.

Truthfully, Elizabeth had felt rejected by me throughout our short marriage, and my admitted lovelessness made her unwilling to keep things as they were. First, she began sleeping in our guest bedroom. Next, she told me she needed a week apart and would be sleeping at a nearby hotel. Finally, at week's end, she informed me she wanted a trial separation of six months and that she was moving in with a friend that lived a few miles away from our house.

First a failure at work, I was now a failure at home too. And just as I had done in my professional life, I sought relief from my marital problems in new and uncharted places. I decided Elizabeth's absence meant I was now a free man and could live however I pleased. I started regularly watching online pornography, and during our six-month trial separation, I had my first three adulterous affairs.

Elizabeth and I never felt totally at peace with getting divorced, and we eventually and mutually agreed for her to move back home so we could give our marriage another shot. As we reconnected, I asked few questions about her activities during the prior six months, perhaps because I didn't want her to ask me about mine, and I didn't tell her about my adulteries. While I was open to our marriage's success, I found it hard to be genuinely hopeful about our future together. Elizabeth and I had fought and disagreed too easily and often during our tumultuous history for me to feel otherwise.

A new chapter in that tumultuous history began just days before my twenty-ninth birthday when Elizabeth handed me a gift bag that was empty save for a positive pregnancy test. As I sat on our couch trying to wrap my mind around this stunning new development, I sensed God wanted me to know two things: First, He made me aware that I had been keeping one eye on the proverbial exits, that I had been preparing to flee at the first sign of marital trouble, and that the exit door was now closed and locked. And second, He was going to teach me how to love.

I surrendered to this new reality and felt more optimistic about the future than I had in years. I was elated when our ultrasound results said we were having a baby boy, who we named Tennyson. Tennyson's arrival immediately deepened my capacity to love, but his arrival also exposed my shame over our fiscal reality.

My desperate need to be successful, to feel accepted, and to belong fueled my risky and unwise financial decisions. Although Elizabeth and I had full-time jobs, I also needed to wait tables four nights a week at a fine dining restaurant just to pay our monthly bills, which included two houses (but three mortgage payments), two brand new cars, plus a mountain of other installment and credit card debts.

I blamed my having to work two jobs on the fact that I had majored in English, *not* on my crazed insistence to look wealthy and successful. I reasoned that if I had only gotten a degree in one of the sciences, then my financial situation would've been much better.

Ever in search of fanciful cures, I decided to explore the possibility of going back to school. I met with an admissions advisor at a local technical college about the fields of nuclear medicine and radiology, which both interested me. At the end of our meeting, I asked the advisor, "Is there any other field you think I should consider?"

She had an immediate answer: "I tell everyone who will listen that they should go to pharmacy school."

Pharmacy school. That was it. I knew that's what I should do. Becoming a pharmacist would guarantee me a six-figure income; it would guarantee me universal acceptance; it would guarantee me the feeling that I belonged.

I immediately put the plans in motion to pursue a degree in pharmacy, and Elizabeth and I packed up our things, and Tennyson, and moved back to our shared hometown of Columbia, South Carolina, in June 2008. I had lived in Myrtle Beach for eight and a half years; Elizabeth for over six. We were mutually ecstatic to leave the beach behind.

FIVE

RECESSION

Elizabeth, Tennyson, and I arrived in Columbia, temporarily living with Elizabeth's sister, brother-in-law, and niece for a few months before ultimately moving into the above-ground basement at my parents' house where I grew up. I began taking pre-pharmacy classes at the University of South Carolina, and I earned a living publishing online articles for a company that sold tickets for sporting and other entertainment events. This job was a lifesaver: it paid incredibly well, I could work from anywhere, and I could craft my work schedule around my classes and family events.

I was in my second semester of taking pre-pharmacy courses when The Great Recession hit, and my lifesaving job writing and publishing online articles was one of the many casualties of the global economic contraction. It was our only source of income since Elizabeth and I had committed to her staying at home to be with Tennyson, who was then two years old.

I would have to find a more traditional way to support my family and pay our bills while I pursued my Doctor of Pharmacy, which was a five-year program. My heart sank as I realized that having a full-time job while being a full-time student would cause me to miss out on those five years of Tennyson's life.

Whether it was fear of failure, parental longing, or pressing financial needs, I decided to surrender my dream of becoming a pharmacist and to re-enter the workforce. I finished my one year of pre-pharmacy classes with a 3.4 GPA, which I liked to round up to 4.

The Great Recession in 2009 marked the most intense period of economic uncertainty that I had experienced in my life. I began listening to economics podcasts like Bloomberg Surveillance so that I could hear the opinions of financial experts. I started to believe that I could finally create the financial liberty I had so desperately craved by trading stocks. I borrowed $25 thousand and tried my hand at the markets during the day and waited tables at Ruth's Chris at night.

The hope of getting rich trading stocks was a delicious elixir. I used the elixir to avoid facing the reality that our monthly debt load was unsustainable. I used it to avoid facing my sadness and shame over having decided to drop out of school. I used it to avoid feeling depressed that Elizabeth, Tennyson, and I had moved in with my parents because we couldn't afford to live on our own.

I had great success trading stocks in the market until the unimaginable happened and I lost eighty percent of my trading capital over a soul-sucking period of four days. The dream of getting rich in the stock market had been the sweetest and most intoxicating dream I had ever known, but that sweet and intoxicating dream had ended, and I was now waking up to my painful reality.

I was a thirty-three-year-old husband and father of two boys under the age of five—our second son, Asher, was born in 2010—who waited tables in a fine dining restaurant while living in his parents' basement. I could no longer pay the mountain of debts that I had incurred. I had bankrupted our family, and Elizabeth and I publicly declared as much in 2011. This was a new low.

The news wasn't all bad, though. We were attending a small church plant led by people we had met while living in Myrtle Beach, and church leaders asked me to help lead worship. Of course, I didn't tell them about my habit of watching online pornography or that I had been unfaithful to Elizabeth a couple more times since having three affairs back in 2005.

In my role as the worship leader, I crossed paths with a man who was the director of a local business. He mentioned he had an opening at his company, and he invited me to interview, which I did. He offered me a job, and I accepted, bringing my number of employers to three: I had an office job during the day, waited tables at Ruth's Chris on the weekends, and led worship at church on Sundays.

The combined monthly income from my three jobs was just enough to allow us to afford a small monthly rent. We moved out of my parents' basement and into the home of Elizabeth's parents, which was vacant since they lived overseas. Even though we were renting from Elizabeth's parents and could only afford to live there because her parents graciously charged us a low monthly rent, it was nice to have a place to ourselves.

As the calendar year turned to 2012, I was nothing like the man I had hoped or planned to be. I felt mortally and hopelessly ashamed of all that I'd yet to achieve, and I spent most of my time and energy regretting the choices I had made in the past. I lacked principles, wisdom, and respect for others; and all three of these deficiencies were on full display when I decided to have an affair with a coworker.

SIX

THE JIG IS UP

The year 2012 may go down as the most pivotal year of my life, even though the pivots came out of my having an affair with a coworker. My already shameful decision to commit adultery was made worse by the fact that the coworker and I were also members of the same church. She was a part of the church's main campus, as was the company owner, and I attended and led worship at the downtown campus. So when my campus pastor, who was also an elder, sent me a text out of the blue late one Friday night saying we needed to meet the next morning, I had a feeling that my affair had come to light.

I met with my campus pastor and two other elders on Saturday, August 4, 2012. The meeting started with one of the men looking at me and saying, "Well, I guess the jig is up."

And so it was.

The elders said I had been accused of committing adultery with a coworker, and at that moment, sitting in a small office in an otherwise empty church with my back against the wall, I felt like a cornered fugitive who had finally been caught and was now overcome with exhaustion after spending a decade on the run. I knew lying was pointless so I gave myself up. I confessed that the accusation of adultery was true.

Confessing my adultery to the elders was a pivotal moment for me, for deceit begets darkness while honesty begets the light. Being honest with the elders allowed me to start being honest with myself for the first time in years, and as I opened up about my past and honestly answered the elders' questions about my history of sexual sins, the three men and I learned together just how desolate my life had become.

I knew there'd be consequences for my actions, and there were. The elders informed me that I'd been fired from the company where the affair occurred and that I'd have to resign from the role of worship leader at church effective immediately. But they also forced me to face my greatest fear by asking if I thought Elizabeth would leave me after she learned about the affair. I said I didn't think she would, but that I didn't know for certain. And I explained that I wouldn't know her reaction for hours, because as fate would have it, she and the boys were in Myrtle Beach attending the birthday party of some dear friends and wouldn't get home until late that night.

Even though I knew there'd be consequences for my actions, facing them, and knowing there were more to come, left me in a state of shock. By the time my meeting with the elders was over, I was physically and mentally drained, but emotionally, I was more alive than I'd been in years.

Revealing parts of myself to the elders that I'd kept hidden for decades had unexpectedly awakened and mobilized a heap of thoughts and feelings that I'd banished long ago. As I got in my car and began the drive home, these thoughts and feelings began marching toward me, demanding my attention.

I thought about the years I'd wasted offering people false versions of myself hoping to be accepted, with nothing to show for my efforts but a trail of damaged relationships and unpaid debts. I wondered how my life might've been different had I spent those same years learning to accept, embrace, and develop the real me.

I felt sad to have spent the better part of three decades rejecting myself. I'd always kept the real me hidden in the dark, promising myself I could come out and be seen once I had been magically transformed into a person that everyone would accept and love. The dream of being magically transformed consumed me, and I used it as a means to substitute fantasy for reality.

The fantasy of being magically transformed allowed me to dismiss Elizabeth's agony over the state of our marriage by imagining myself becoming the man she'd always craved. It allowed me to reframe our financial ruin and eventual bankruptcy as mere struggles to endure before striking it rich. And it allowed me to shrug off how I had wronged and hurt people by picturing myself as the man those same people would one day come to admire and adore.

But as I continued driving home and neared my house, I noticed reality was unapologetically reclaiming the places in my life where I had let fantasy reign.

I pulled into our empty driveway and killed the engine, staggered to the front door, and let myself in. The house was filled with ominous silence, and this silence allowed my reckoning to commence and continue without the threat of interruption.

I paced the house in emotional agony as a montage of affair partners, lies, and ways I had betrayed Elizabeth played on a continual loop in my mind. The parade of images and old memories produced a shame and sorrow that flooded me and washed out all vestiges of self-righteousness like water hollows a stone.

Everywhere I looked I saw something that pierced my heart anew: a family photo, the postcard under a magnet on the fridge that was a friendly reminder of an upcoming doctor's appointment, a picture colored by the kids, or a toy left out in the middle of the floor.

I tried to escape the pain by going to sleep, but I found that my dreams were synched with my waking mind and played the same images. I laid in Tennyson's vacated bed and drank in his leftover scent. I realized how badly I did not want to lose him. Or Asher. Or Elizabeth. Or our house. Or our years together. Or this room, or those toys, or these blankets on this bed. I wept in anguish because I had realized this too late.

Elizabeth and the boys returned home late that evening. As she and I got ready for bed, I confessed the adultery, and I told her about the meeting with the elders and that I had been fired from the two jobs. Seeing her anger, sadness, and deep disappointment was the worst moment in a day filled with horrible moments. As I laid awake listening to her sobs, I resigned myself to the fact that whether she divorced me or not, I would spend the rest of my days living as an undesired, unacceptable man.

Saturday, August 4, 2012, is not my birthdate. It's the day I came into being. It's the day I went from being married to being a husband, from having kids to being a dad, and from being a shadow of a self to being a real person. I think of that unforgettable day as "the begisding," for the beginning of the new and ending of the old were separated by a thin and unclear line. The new and the old are forever and inextricably linked; birth and death share a common waiting room; life and loss split off from the same lobby. Just when the life I had always known was ending, a life I could not imagine was beginning.

PART TWO

GLEANED TO GLEAM

"Behold, you delight in truth
in the inward being . . ."

PSALM 51:6A ESV

SEVEN

BOMBARDIER

My confession to Elizabeth, both of my marital unfaithfulness as well as the job losses and resultant economic difficulties, made me feel like a bombardier who detonated a hydrogen bomb right over the top of his house. Our already tenuous hopes and dreams and relationships and finances were blown to bits and replaced by a massive crater with scorched walls and floor.

Only three things survived the hydrogen bomb's blast: the real me, who I didn't want; my wife and kids, who might not want me; and my waiter job at Ruth's Chris, which had become a dire necessity, a fact that humiliated me to the bone.

The hydrogen bomb event transformed our house into a kind of bomb shelter. While being in the shelter was hard, leaving the shelter to venture out into the world was harder.

Activities that had been the mere drudgeries of life before the bomb were now the only reasons Elizabeth and I left the shelter at all. We had to eat, so we had to go get food, so we showered and had to take off our old, dirty clothes and put on new, fresh, clean ones. We didn't leave the bomb shelter because we could. We left because we had to.

Then again, nearly everything Elizabeth and I did in the hours, days, and weeks following the bomb's detonation was done because we had to, and one of the things I had to do was to face the strange, postnuclear world I had created.

The hydrogen bomb's blast had instantly and violently fused my secret and public lives, which meant that I had to face and own the damage I had done with little place to hide. For a man who had been hiding for over a decade, having almost nowhere to hide made already hard things feel impossible.

There were impossible conversations, such as the one with extended family in our bomb shelter when I hinted that "personal issues" had cost me my nine-to-five salaried job as well as my position of worship leader at church and that I'd be waiting tables a few more nights a week to make ends meet.

I had conversations like this over and over with family and non-family alike, and not a single person understood why a thirty-five-year-old husband and father of two children under five would do such a thing. Everyone sensed there was more to the story and demanded more details, but they weren't going to get it from me. Not at that time.

The truth comes whole and can't be sliced into acceptable, comfortable pieces. What my mouth refused to confess, my heart was forced to suffer. When people asked me why I wasn't leading worship, I'd say that I just needed a break, while my heart relived my meeting with the three elders and my admitted infidelity. When people asked me how Elizabeth was, I'd say she's doing well, while my heart relived my confession to her and the tears, anger, and hurt it produced.

My refusal to bear the whole truth aloud made these conversations unbearable. It made my whole life feel unbearable. But little did I know then, my days of refusing to bear the whole truth were numbered.

EIGHT

SEX ADDICT

Back during my meeting with the three elders, I had inadvertently blurted out that unless I got help, I was sure I would cheat again. A few days after the meeting, one of the elders gave me the contact info for someone named Dee. The elder said I should contact Dee, that she could help me, and that she'd have me take an assessment.

At the time the elder gave me Dee's info, I felt hopelessly ashamed and didn't see what I stood to lose by calling her. Plus, I liked the idea of taking an assessment, assuming it was like those Facebook personality quizzes or vocational assessments that helped people understand why they hadn't reached their full potential and how they could unlock their inner champion.

I called Dee and got her voicemail; she called me back and got mine. I listened to her message. She said I would need to schedule an in-office appointment so she could evaluate whether I should take the online assessment for sexually addictive behavior. Sex addiction?! The phrase knocked the wind out of me.

"There's no way I'm a sex addict!" I thought.

I went and looked at myself in the mirror to make sure I didn't *look* like a sex addict, and then I went and lay down. My mind was racing.

"Yes, I admit I've made mistakes," I thought.

"And I'm obviously bad at relationships," I continued.

"But that doesn't mean I'm a sex addict," I reasoned.

"Aren't sex addicts great with women?" I wondered.

"My kingdom to be great with women!" I joked but realized that none of this was funny.

I was offended and outraged, especially at the elder who recommended I call Dee but didn't tell me that the assessment was to determine whether I was a sex addict. I scheduled my first appointment with her and looked forward to clearing up this little misunderstanding.

Delores "Dee" Parlato was a middle-aged woman with dark hair mixed with gray. Her bio said she retired from the U.S. Navy, where she spent twenty years as a photojournalist, and that she was now a licensed counselor and trained spiritual director. I sat down on her couch and was immediately unsettled by how she appeared to see through me. She had a practiced posture of neutrality; she would reserve judgment until *she* felt ready to judge, and her judgment could not be bought. She questioned me about my sexual history and took notes on a legal pad of yellow paper.

"Did I view internet pornography?" "How often?" "When did I start?" "Had I ever tried to stop?" "Had I ever been involved in an extramarital affair?" "How many times?" "Who were my affair partners?"

We had moved on from the affairs when I remembered another one, and I interrupted her so it could be added to the list. I felt proud for offering up this extra sin, and I hoped Dee would be moved by my courage. She listened intently as I summarized the forgotten adultery, and when I stopped talking, she took off her glasses and put down her pen.

"*How could you forget something like that?*" she asked incredulously.

Her words were ice cold and her gaze red hot, and she seemed truly disgusted with me. Her question pierced through the remaining layers of my false self, and I felt utterly ashamed.

Dee recommended I take the 500+ question assessment for sexually addictive behavior. I took it and returned to her office a couple of weeks later to go over the results. Dee and I sat across from each other as we had during our first session together, but I had my guards up and on high alert this time.

Dee started the session by saying the assessment results pointed to sexually addictive or compulsive behavior. She went through my results across the spectrum of categories, and my self-disgust grew with her every word. In short, I was a "sex addict," which, in my mind, made me a clinically certified piece of shit.

A "sex addict" can be described as a person who has a compulsive need to perform sexual acts such as masturbation, viewing pornography, or being in sexually stimulating situations. The sex addict uses sexually acting out as a way to achieve the kind of "relief" that an alcoholic gets from a drink.

Learning how a sex addict can be defined in no way excused my actions or spared me from suffering the consequences of those actions. Being a Christian, I didn't *have* to sin; I chose to, and I chose to knowing full well that I was placing myself and those I cared about in jeopardy. I disregarded how my actions would hurt and harm the people in my life. I was crestfallen, and I knew I needed help.

Dee ended our second session by offering me the chance to participate in a six-month out-patient treatment program for sex addicts that she founded. The program consisted of a weekly two-hour group therapy session that would meet on Tuesday nights from 6–8 p.m. at the First Presbyterian Christian Counseling Center in Columbia, South Carolina. The group would be made up of nine men including me, and each man had to commit to the following:

- Attending each Tuesday night group session
- Going to at least one Sexaholics Anonymous meeting per week, and
- Completing all assigned readings and worksheets

There were also spiritual exercises we had to do weekly, and there would be two Saturdays where we would be together for eight hours doing deep, exploratory work.

My first group therapy session was on February 19, 2013. The nine men sat in a circle along with Dee and another therapist. Each man's path into the room was different, but we were all convinced that our real self was unacceptable.

The nine of us were all fluent in the language of the self but had only been shown the negatives. Some people are taught "to be," but we had been taught how "not to be." Our families of origin and early influencers had drilled the negatives into us until we had mastered them. We knew "I'm not," "you aren't," "he-she-it isn't," "we aren't," and "they aren't" by heart. We were more comfortable with dishonesty than honesty, felt unloved more than loved, and knew how to be immoral and inappropriate better than moral and appropriate.

The group sessions gave us the chance to learn a new language. To add the unfamiliar positives to the deadly familiar negatives and to become fluent speakers. But there was a catch: we'd have to come out of hiding, embrace our real selves, and learn to live in the light. It was a chance we were all willing to take.

Our sessions had all the elements of a typical introductory language course. The ebb and flow of hope and disappointment: believing we could do it one minute but not the next, feeling anger toward those who hadn't made us learn the language in the past and resentment toward those who were making us learn it now, wondering if we were too old to learn a new language, mourning the lost years, feeling both proud and ashamed to be learning it now.

The group gave me tools to express myself more fully, honestly, and precisely. It's where I first realized and then put words around the idea that "the real me is unacceptable." While invisible, this idea had dominated and nearly destroyed my life. Naming it had the mysterious effect of letting me see it everywhere it had previously gone undetected and unchallenged. Like when someone pointed out the arrow between the "E" and "x" in the FedEx logo, I would never again be able to *not* see it.

The group was life-changing but not life-curing. I had spent six months practicing this new language, learning how to live as my real self, and how not to use sex addiction to numb my pain. Now it was time to use it out in the real world, and I would learn the hard way that proficiency in the classroom is way different from mastery in the streets.

NINE

BUILDING AND BOMBING

My life's singular focus was slowly and painstakingly rebuilding the hopes and dreams and relationships and finances that had been destroyed by the hydrogen bomb of my moral failures. The crater with scorched walls and floor, which memorialized my bomb's detonation, remained. But now there were important structures of stability rising around it.

I completed the six-month group treatment program, and I was regularly going to my twelve-step meetings. I was still seeing Dee for individual therapy, and she had me working on the pièce de résistance of the recovery world: the "disclosure," which is the structured process wherein the addict confesses and takes responsibility for everything they've done in the way of sexually acting out.

Elizabeth had been gracious to me; she hadn't left me nor asked me to leave. I'd been given another chance. We had unintentionally gotten pregnant shortly after the bomb, and we'd welcomed a healthy and beautiful baby girl into our family. We'd survived the horrific explosion and seemed to have emerged from it stronger. Elizabeth saw the work I was putting in and how I was striving to improve. I was trying to live honestly and with integrity, and to no longer hide the real me. I was sober and now able to see and think more clearly.

Life was getting better, and each day seemed to put a little more distance between me and my cratered past. But the crater would always be with me, and the best I could hope for was to build a better life around the crater and to always remember that while building and bombing were equally possible, they didn't have to be equally *probable*. I wasn't planning to return to my addictive and sexually compulsive ways after investing hundreds of hours and thousands of dollars in my recovery and personal growth, and I couldn't imagine ever again being the heartless bastard that betrayed the trust and spurned the love of his own family and closest friends.

The company where I had previously held my nine-to-five salaried position rehired me to work remotely and in a different capacity. I was thankful for this, but I also felt compelled to see if there might be any degrees, licenses, or certifications that would create more and better opportunities for me in the future without taking years to obtain. It so happened that the company wanted me to get my residential mortgage loan originator's license, and this seemed like the perfect solution. I prepared for the various exams and earned my South Carolina license.

I started working in this new capacity and got a promotion and a pay raise. In my new role, I worked closely with a girl in a different department who I'd considered a good work friend before my scandalous exit and who'd been supportive and kind since my return. We had similar tastes in music, movies, and humor. We vented work frustrations and tried to encourage each other. We also would joke about sex and enjoyed the double entendre, but the jokes were always about sex in general and not about each other. She never came on to me nor did I ever make advances toward her, and since our jokes and comments hadn't been directed at each other, I thought she couldn't be offended. But one Friday in November 2013 I learned that she could be offended and that I had said something she found offensive.

She had reported me to her supervisor, who reported me to the company director, who reported me to the company's in-house legal counsel, who reported me to the owner and was now seated across from me in the conference room notifying me of her accusation and the company's formal response.

I was nonplussed. I absolutely did not mean to offend her, but I absolutely did. *I could not believe this was happening again.*

The first time I got in trouble at work for sexually acting out, I was fully aware of the bomb I was building; I'd just hoped I could keep it from exploding. This time, I didn't see the bomb at all. I didn't say a word during the meeting with the in-house counsel; I was too busy dying inside. I knew I'd be fired again, but I now knew something else that was far, far worse.

While my body was in the room with the company esquire, my heart, mind, and soul were taking a Dickensian trip led by the Ghosts of Addiction Past, Present, and Yet To Come. The Ghost of Addiction Past took me back to when I first started acting out and showed me the succession of boundaries I had crossed and people I'd betrayed. I watched how my sinful urges grew in both depth and breadth over time. I could see my younger self begging God for help while promising to change, only to act out again days or even hours later.

The Ghost of Addiction Present showed me the events of August 4, 2012, followed by some of the highlights from the group therapy treatment program I had completed. I saw people being proud of the progress I had made, then I saw me making the offensive comment to my coworker and my lifeless walk to the room I was now in.

The Ghost of Addiction Yet To Come showed me working at one prestigious and high-paying job after the other and getting fired from each one because of inappropriate sexual behaviors. Finally, I saw myself as an old, grayed, feeble man who was utterly alone because of a lifetime of having chosen lust over real people.

My trip complete, I was right back in the conference room. While the lawyer talked, I focused on what had become crystal clear to me: I was for sure a sex addict, I was completely powerless over lust, and my life had become unmanageable. I finally understood that there was no job I could not lose, no salary I would not squander, and no position I could not desecrate through my sexually addictive behavior.

And unfortunately, the author of my story is no Charles Dickens. The heavy and uncomfortable realization that I was unhealthy and hopelessly addicted to lust couldn't be undone and remade during a twenty-four-hour spree of do-gooding and right-making. I would have to sit in my sickness and addiction until I was ready and able to crawl, and I would have to think not of total cures but rather of taking the next right steps.

My meeting with in-house counsel occurred late on a Friday afternoon, and I entered the weekend having been suspended indefinitely. By the following Monday, I still hadn't told Elizabeth what happened, partly because I wasn't officially terminated but mostly because I wouldn't bring myself to tell her.

Knowing and rejecting the idea that "the real me is unacceptable" was far different from knowing and embracing the "real me," especially when the "real me" had been fired twice in fifteen months from the same company for sexually inappropriate behavior.

Lacking the courage to offer Elizabeth my real self, I hid inside the large public library downtown during the hours I would have normally been at work, and I hoped I wouldn't see anyone Elizabeth and I knew. I also hoped Elizabeth wouldn't ask me any questions I was afraid to answer; to be such a contemptuous and unfaithful person, I had always been a terrible liar.

I noticed one tiny yet remarkable change in myself during this experience: hiding the real me prohibited my being fully present with Elizabeth, and this felt unpleasant and painful. For the first time in forever, I saw that hiding the real me *produced* pain; I had always believed that hiding the real me would either reduce my pain or eliminate it entirely.

I finally told Elizabeth about my work violation later that week, just before receiving official notice that I'd been terminated. She barely responded to the news. I had betrayed her so many times during our marriage that she now almost came to expect it.

TEN

WHOLE 30

After having been fired a second time for inappropriate sexual behaviors, I spent the next few days and weeks in a state of shock, unsure of what to do moving forward. I kept wondering how my moral corruptness could resurface within three months of completing my group treatment program, and the fact that I didn't have an answer made me feel desperate and willing to try anything. I had been introduced to new spiritual exercises during my group therapy, and one was the practice of silence and solitude, which I just called silence.

I'd found practicing silence to be the best and most rewarding way to learn about myself, which was ironic, because silence had been my mortal enemy during the years I spent searching for the acceptable me. The real me did not want to be replaced, and I realized that he would never, and could never, be silenced. The real me would always beg me not to replace him, so I bound and gagged him before leaving for my search. Despite the years of suppression and distance between us, I would hear his familiar mumbled pleas the moment I was quiet and still, and my only recourse was to drown him out through external noise and constant movement.

I was supposed to have spent at least thirty minutes in silence each week I was in the program, but I'd never done the full thirty in a single sitting.

"Why not spend thirty minutes in silence now?" I wondered.

I drove down to the Three Rivers Greenway on a cloudy afternoon and found an empty wooden bench overlooking the Congaree River. I sat down, opened my phone's timer, and spun the wheel until it read "30 min." I took a deep, deep breath, pressed "Start," and closed my eyes.

I entered silence in a state of surrender. The belief that doing something different *might* produce something different comforted me, though I was too weary and beleaguered to have unspoken hopes or fears about what I'd encounter. I just sat still.

My attention eventually drifted to my upcoming disclosure and I floated there in tow. I was surprised to find myself willing to engage my thoughts and feelings, whatever they were; I was surprised to feel unafraid and even brave.

I realized that disclosure offered me a rare and truly special opportunity to be known. I was weeks away from my twelfth wedding anniversary, and I'd hid my real self from Elizabeth for most of those years. I wondered what our marriage might have been had I offered her my real self then; I wondered what our marriage may look like in another twelve years if I started offering my real self to her now. This idea put wind in my sails. I felt encouraged but also knew that offering my real self to her required complete honesty. I wanted to be sure the disclosure included everything.

Having been fired days earlier for sexually compulsive behavior at work, it was fresh on my mind, and I decided to think through every job I'd had since graduating college to see if there was anything else that belonged in the disclosure. There was. I even remembered an affair I'd *tried* to have but didn't because of a scheduling conflict. The affair was prevented by a calendar, not my character, and Elizabeth deserved to know about this, too. I did the same exercise for everywhere I'd lived after graduating from college, for every trip I had taken, and for every place I had visited.

"Ring!" My alarm sounded, and I was bungeed from deep within myself back to the bench overlooking the Congaree. Re-examining where I had worked, lived, and visited had been incredibly productive, allowing me to dredge up what would be another five typed pages of previously forgotten material I would get to disclose to Elizabeth in less than a month.

"Wow!" I exclaimed quietly.

I couldn't believe what had just taken place. My life hadn't changed one speck during the last thirty minutes, yet I felt radically different. I didn't feel superhuman; I felt real and human, and it felt good and just right. I also felt the presence of something that was both strange and familiar: *gratitude*. I felt grateful to be myself and have my life—fortunate even! I wouldn't trade either of them for all the world.

I had questions—lots of them. I had spent thirty minutes poring over my most shameful acts. How did I now feel unashamed? I'd confronted so much personal weakness. How did I now feel strong and even valiant? I'd acknowledged decades of self-betrayal. How was I now able to love and embrace the real me?

At that moment, I didn't know and I didn't care. I hadn't felt these slivers of strength, valiance, and self-love since becoming a Christian at eighteen years old, and being able to feel them again now was good enough for me.

ELEVEN

NEXT RIGHT STEP

T hanks to my magical time of silence sitting by the Congaree River, I was able to prepare a more thorough and rigorously honest disclosure. While the magic didn't include making the disclosure feel *easy*, I was able to take comfort from knowing that telling the truth was the best way to honor Elizabeth and, ironically, myself.

The day finally came for me to share my disclosure with Elizabeth. Dee moderated as I slowly and carefully read the thirteen typed pages detailing the ways I had betrayed Elizabeth through my sexually addictive behavior, including the affairs, whether physical or emotional, the pornography, and the lies. I also acknowledged how my sexually addictive behavior had led to our relational instability, financial hardships, and generally toxic family environment. Sharing my disclosure with Elizabeth was the hardest thing I had ever done.

Elizabeth had known in advance that she would benefit from having some physical space to process what she would hear, so we had planned to sleep in different rooms for a while following the disclosure. She and I kept our lines of communication open and eschewed the making of concrete plans of the future for living one day at a time.

For me, living one day at a time meant focusing on taking the next right step. I was still waiting tables at Ruth's Chris and still going to my twelve-step meetings for sex addicts. I had even started and completed what's referred to as "90 in 90," which is attending ninety in-person or phone meetings over ninety consecutive days.

After one in-person meeting, a fellow addict came up to me and said, "I heard you say you had your mortgage loan originator's license. Are you looking to stay in that business? Is that what you want to do?"

I told him I thought I did want to stay in the loan origination business, and he offered to put me in touch with a couple of people he knew. I was grateful for his willingness to do that for me, though I was anxious about meeting with experienced, qualified people when I was so inexperienced and felt so unqualified. While it was true I was a licensed originator, I'd yet to close a single loan and I wasn't sure if anyone would want to hire me.

During this period of uncertainty, I repeatedly asked God to tell me exactly what I should do about work. He hadn't. But anytime I prayed or thought about my work future, the same specific image would come to mind: I was a child in the deep end of a pool. I had on those inflatable armbands (I always called them swimmies), but I wasn't sure if they'd be able to keep my head above water. Also, there was a man in the deep end of the pool, less than an arm's length away from me. The man wasn't someone I recognized, yet he also felt strangely familiar. The man kept his eyes on me, but he wouldn't hold me. I got the impression that I would have to learn whether the swimmies could keep me from drowning. If not, I'd find out whether the man next to me would notice I'd gone under; if so, I'd see if he was willing and able to pull my head back above the water so I could breathe.

The message was clear: whether I stayed in the mortgage business or worked in an entirely different field, I would have to swim in the deep end of the pool.

My friend kept his word and introduced me to two people in the mortgage business, and I interviewed with both. They asked me questions about my ability to connect and build relationships with people, and the only experiences I could reference were from Ruth's Chris, where I had more previous guests specifically request me as their server than anyone else on the wait staff.

But steaks aren't mortgages, and it required someone to be able to see how my current success in one area might predict future success in the other. The second person that interviewed me made that connection, and he offered me a job several days after our interview. I nervously accepted.

I had told my future boss during the interview that I had no idea whether I'd succeed or how long it might take. The very nature of the job pushed every insecurity button I had: it was straight commission; I had to keep offering myself and my services to people who probably didn't know me; I would be told "no" dozens or even hundreds of times for every time I was told "yes," and now real and large dollars were attached to this rejection or acceptance, which played and preyed upon my fears of not being able to provide for my family. I knew the practice of silence would play an even bigger role in my life, so I told my new boss, "If you know I'm here but see my door closed with the lights off, I'm sitting in silence and will be out after a while."

I closed one loan during my first six months. I was only able to feed my family by asking my elderly mom and dad for money. I only endured life's uncertainties by sitting in silence on an almost-daily basis. During these times of silence, God met me and showed me unimaginable things, things that defied space and time, things too marvelous to be properly conveyed by any language.

TWELVE

CRATER OF SHAME

I started my new job in March 2014. On my first day, I realized I left something I needed at the house, and I asked Elizabeth to drop it off for me. When she arrived, I invited her to come inside to see my office and to meet my coworkers. As I walked her back out to the car, she whispered, "I think this is the healthiest place you've ever worked." She noticed how my new coworkers were all people of faith and were kind, humble, encouraging, and accustomed to success.

I was building up another structure of stability, and now my crater—which memorialized my shameful past and moral failures—was almost completely obscured. In my mind, the only potential clues that pointed to my shameful history were my age, inexperience, and lack of success. Why else would a thirty-seven-year-old be starting a new job in what was essentially a new career?

I desperately wanted the immediate removal of anything that might connect me to my crater. I wanted to ensure that no one would know about it ever again unless *I wanted* them to. I assumed there were people whose lives were crater free, but the rest of us had to hope in the world's beatitude, which says, **"Blessed are those who hide their craters well, for they shall be called craterless."**

My battle for crater invisibility was fought inside my warm, comfortable office at work. I called realtors and individuals I knew, and the momentum for or against my crater's obscurity would swing based on how the call went. Some people I called seemed so otherworldly successful that I'd hang up convinced they knew I had a crater while I knew they did not, and therefore they'd never want to do business with someone like me. I was hopelessly envious of these vocational masters who, by comparison, made me feel so shabby and unimpressive. But other calls gave me hope that with just a little more time and a little luck I'd enjoy enough success to hide my crater for good, and I'd hang up excited and anxious for that day to come.

Some calls and certain outcomes would stir me up profoundly, and whenever I had feelings that I either didn't understand or didn't know how to process, I would shut my office door, turn off my lights, and sit with God in silence for fifteen minutes.

During these times I learned to pay attention to what I felt. But more importantly, I learned to parse my feelings to find what was most true, which often differed from what was loudest, most available, or overwhelming.

There were many times I sat with God in silence and nothing noteworthy happened; I merely benefitted from being still and quiet and from offering myself to Him as honestly as I knew how.

Other times I gained significant insights and clarity around what I was feeling and why I was feeling it, and those times were amazing.

But at some point, I started noticing a subtle change when I sat with God in silence: He began to direct my attention to my crater of shame, the epicenter of my moral failures. I didn't want to think about my crater of shame. I wanted to forget about it and for it to be permanently invisible to others. But I felt I had to at least look at whatever He showed me since I was coming to Him for help, like streaming a free show but you have to watch the ads.

Whenever God focused His attention on my crater, it didn't feel like He was trying to be rude or ugly or to hurt me. It seemed He was just letting me know that He knew it was there and that it was important to Him. Occasionally, it seemed like He was asking if I'd go with Him to my crater—would I be willing to look at it, face it, own it, and discuss it?

This I didn't care for, or understand, or trust. I didn't know why He'd even ask me to go there when He knew the crater's mere presence had caused me to feel such tremendous pain. I felt sure He would only ask if *He* had something to gain, and I assumed His gain would come at *my* expense. So, I refused to entertain the offer or to talk with God about it anymore. And then came the perfect storm.

One day, I was sitting alone with God in silence, and I was furious and fed up with Him. For months, I had asked God over and over to bless my business, yet I'd only closed one measly loan, and I was sick and tired of groveling to my elderly mom and dad before asking them for money so I could feed my family and pay the bills. I felt ashamed and I resented it, and I intended to give God a piece of my mind. I was looking for a fight.

My defenses were up, and I started in on Him with a series of questions I hoped would force Him to at least engage me, if not act on my behalf: "Would it be too much for You to care a little?

Are You just too busy to lift a finger to help me? Do You have it too good to be bothered by me? Or do you just enjoy watching me suffer?"

He didn't respond to a single question, much less fight back. It was like I hadn't said a word, which infuriated me further.

"Will you go with Me to your crater?" He asked, as calmly as ever.

I was taken aback when He responded and doubly so when I heard His question. I had anticipated that if He engaged me at all, it would be to defend Himself; His approach caught me totally off guard and momentarily disarmed me.

But anger quickly regained its foothold and I answered His question with as much venomous sarcasm as I could muster, "Oh, I'd *love* to."

We set off for my crater. I used the travel time to try and figure out what God was up to and why He was so intent on us going to my crater together. Unable to know His plan for certain, I settled on the theory I found most likely given what others had taught me about God.

This was my theory: God had been waiting patiently for the perfect moment to unleash His judgment and anger on me for my mistakes and moral failures. And with the crater being the epicenter of my shame, it was the perfect place, the place His rejection of me would hurt the most. God wanted to be the last one in line to give me my comeuppance, and He looked forward to going down my list of sins confronting me about each one and, upon my confession of guilt, would point out the exact chapter and verse where He'd forbidden it.

God and I soon arrived at my crater, and from where we stood I could see the crater's entire scorched and radioactive terrain, still charred black and devoid of life. Seeing the crater affected me the same way every time: I felt as if a literal ton of guilt, sorrow, and shame was placed on my chest, taking my breath away.

God and I stood there quietly. I felt the full weight of my mistakes, and I couldn't bring myself to look at Him. I waited for Him to make the first move.

"Is there any life here?" He asked after some time, though the answer was painfully obvious.

"No," I replied, using up the last little bit of defensiveness I'd retained.

Then He asked, "*Can there be* life here?"

"No," I answered dejectedly, after quite a long pause.

His second question broke me. He had used it to pinpoint the specific fear that had haunted me the most: that my heinous behavior and shameful choices had done permanent and irrevocable damage; that my relationships with others could never be mended; that I could never again even be trusted, much less loved.

This was the significance of the crater's scorched and radioactive terrain. It represented how my crater had masterfully engineered the space to be uninhabitable to all but itself, uninhabitable to anything good and alive, uninhabitable to all but guilt, remorse, and shame. I was convinced that if I were to live another ten million years, the crater would be just as scorched and radioactive and devoid of life then as it was at this very moment.

As these thoughts whirred within me, I kept my eyes to the ground, being too ashamed to do anything or to look anywhere else. But I knew we couldn't leave until I received what God had reserved for me, so I finally looked over at Him.

I expected to find on His face expressions ranging from sadness and disappointment to anger and contempt, but I didn't. Instead, His face expressed a deep and abiding love, and His eyes beamed with fire and ferocity. His face and His eyes rendered me speechless, and I could only stare at Him in wonder and disbelief.

Just then, He looked to the crater's epicenter, where the hydrogen bomb's impact had been most catastrophic. I followed His gaze and watched as a green shoot slowly and reverently emerged from the scorched and radioactive floor. It grew with indifference to my abhorrent past and present shame until it had become a blossoming tree. God had called forth life in the very place where death had previously reigned, and life had obeyed.

I looked at God a second time, filled now with even greater wonder and with even more disbelief, and again I saw fire and ferocity in His eyes. The fire was the kind that warms you to perfection after a long day out in the cold and that delights in your comfort and joy, but never your hurt or fear. I had the feeling that while this fire may leap out against one who meant me harm, it would never leap out against me or harm me.

The ferocity too was there for my good. He was ferocious in His support of me, ferocious in His desire to bless, ferocious in His promise to protect, ferocious in His defense, ferocious in His vigilance against all that would threaten me, and ferocious in His unbreakable commitment that evil not befall or overcome me. The fire and ferocity were forged from love, and they were pure, untainted by hidden motives or selfish gain.

I had many questions, and the only answer He gave me was to a question I didn't ask: God's favor is reserved for the real me—for the man I *really* am—not for the man I want to be. The gift of being honest before Him and of admitting shame is one that only my real self can open.

God met a man at a crater; God met a woman at a well. He chose the place, the time, and the topic that exposed their deepest pain. He addressed the man's shame blamed on women, as He had done with the woman's blamed on men; they both knew lying was pointless. The man and the woman were honest and admitted their shame, and God replaced their misery with a tree, living water, and grace.

THIRTEEN

RADIANT JOY

What I experienced with God at my crater filled me with wonder, and that feeling only grew in the days that were to come. The grace, love, and kindness God bestowed upon me had certainly been amazing. But what astounded me more than God's choice to bless me was realizing that He had also been the one who had prepared me to receive.

Do you think it was due to my courage and merit that I decided to travel to my crater and reconcile with my sordid past? Not a chance! I dealt with my crater of shame by not dealing with it at all, and the best outcome I could imagine was being able to hide my crater so well that other people assumed I was craterless.

I only went to my crater because God kept asking me to go. I was only honest before Him because His questions pierced my heart and I no longer wanted to lie. And because of God's presence, admitting my shame became as desirable as hiding it had always been. So my crater, which had always overwhelmed me, because of God, had been overcome.

The wondrous and incredible experience I'd shared with God at my crater had momentarily filled me with great joy, but that joy was soon snuffed out by my financial and material needs. I was months into my job as a mortgage loan originator where I was paid solely on commission, and I couldn't support my family with an empty pipeline. What would bring me great joy, I thought, would be figuring out how to convert that incredible experience into cold hard cash I could then use to buy gas and groceries!

I was embarrassed about my finances, but I couldn't say I was surprised. God had warned me before I even took this job that, whether I was a mortgage loan originator or something completely different, I'd have to learn to swim in the deep end of the pool. But with the water now up to my nose, I feared I was about to drown.

The fear was bad, but what humiliated me even more was having to admit that I was too scared to even try to swim. I was overwhelmed with fear, and I felt paralyzed in the pool, unable to paddle my arms or kick my legs.

I sat with God in silence because I could do nothing else, and God chose to reveal Himself and remind me He could do all things.

Looking back, it makes sense that this time of silence with God would be different. I no longer feared being honest before God, not after what I had experienced at the crater. Of course, that experience didn't guarantee God would always astound me, but I could be certain He would never condemn me when I offered myself to Him.

I sat in silence, but instead of encountering God, I immediately encountered strong internal resistance. My thoughts asserted that

I was making a big mistake, that sitting in silence was a pointless waste of time, and that I should get back to work and at least give myself a *chance* to better my circumstances.

And still, I sat. I sat, and I faced my anxiety and fear. I admitted to God that I felt frozen, even paralyzed. I admitted I didn't want to drown. And I admitted I was afraid He'd let me.

At some point—though I'm unsure when—God's presence became inescapable. It was all I could see, and it was all I wanted to. His presence reminded me of the sun, but He was colored like the warm and soft-yet-brilliant yellow-orange orbs I would see just after sunrise or just before sunset. I sensed He chose this warm color so I could look on Him; His usual brightness would blind me.

God's presence beamed with radiant joy, and this radiant joy filled me internally and completely enveloped me. God was Himself the source of His joy. He was complete within Himself: He needed nothing. He lacked nothing. He was free to give of Himself to all who had need. His radiant joy was eternal: it had always been, and it would always be.

I sensed I could neither brighten His joy by even a single lumen nor diminish His joy in any way. His radiant joy was independent of my worship and praise, independent of whether I believed He existed at all, independent of whether I thought Him to be good or tyrannous.

But it was impossible to see Him as *anything* other than purely good, impossible to keep my heart from leaping incessantly within me whenever I saw Him or merely thought of Him, and impossible to withhold my most authentic worship and most genuine praise. I offered God my choicest and best words trying to describe His greatness, but my words were unable to properly capture His splendor.

I sat and wept and worshipped. I noticed that even trying to "ascribe to the Lord the glory due His name" (Psalm 29:2) created a virtuous circle: worshipping God deepened and increased my capacity to take in His splendor, which compelled me to worship even more, which deepened my capacity further, and so on.

I sensed that God was infinitely powerful yet infinitely kind, infinitely strong yet infinitely tender. Only God could be arrogant, proud, *and* righteously so, yet He was neither arrogant nor proud. He was glorious in His perfection yet infinitely selfless. His very nature and essence demanded that He give of Himself to all who had need and He would do so forever.

Had it been up to me, I would have stayed in that moment perpetually, simply beholding His radiant joy. But it wasn't up to me. The image changed suddenly and without warning, and I found I was now looking at something like a tiered fountain of pots.

The uppermost pot was the fountain's head, and it continually gushed forth from its unending wellspring of water. It was radiantly joyful and infinitely pleased to pour out from itself and to fill up every pot connected to it. I sensed that God was both the uppermost pot and fountainhead, while the pots underneath and connected to Him were those who were honest before Him.

The fountain could not become exasperated by my needing to be filled, nor could it ever grow weary from pouring out from its fullness to fill my emptiness. The fountain wanted it this way, and it was and would always be. I merely had to be honest and admit I was empty, and the fountain would joyfully fill me again and again, forever.

Once again, the image changed without warning, and I found myself seated at a table covered with otherworldly foods. This time, God took on the appearance of a kind and jovial man. He sat casually across from me, with His back leaned comfortably against the wall at what looked to be an angle of around 110 degrees.

His face beamed with absolute contentment and total satisfaction. He had the look of someone who had just eaten the perfect meal and ate just the right amount so that He could neither be tempted to eat a single bite more nor was repulsed by the sight of food.

He needed nothing and lacked nothing and was free to concentrate His pleasure and wisdom entirely on my experience. He pointed out a food combination that He knew would delight me, and I sensed that this exact pairing would have been inconceivable to me had He not suggested it.

The radiant joy I saw in His face was unaffected by whether I took His suggestion or declined it, and this amazed me. His radiant joy was independent of my choices and whether I trusted Him or not. I could be confident that whatever He offered me was for my benefit, for He was selfless and good, and His motives were unstained and pure. He was incapable of steering me toward a dish because it did not please Him, nor could He steer me away from a dish because He desired it for Himself. I sensed that I alone would suffer by refusing His wisdom, for He would always take joy in His wisdom, whether I took joy in His wisdom or not.

And then it was over.

For some time, I sat in my chair, as tears rolled down my face. I was filled with wonder and unable to speak. When I could, I said aloud, "You are too marvelous for words. You are pure gentility."

And I meant it.

FOURTEEN

WELCOME

I was now the proud owner of two wondrous experiences, but I still suffered embarrassment over having an empty work pipeline. Successful mortgage loan originators build trusted referral partner relationships with realtors, and I searched online for every real estate office in Columbia looking for people I already knew or with whom I had something in common.

One day I came across the name and photo of a realtor I had first met in the seventh grade. She was now married with children, and her husband was also a realtor. I reached out to her, and she remembered me. We had a great conversation, and I ended the call by inviting her and her husband to lunch.

I treated the couple to lunch at Libby's, a small restaurant in Lexington, South Carolina. We had a wonderful time over lunch, laughing and catching up on each other's lives. The lunch went so well, in fact, that the husband called me while I was driving back to my office and said he had a client he wanted to refer to me. I was elated but also terrified!

Whenever I made a positive connection with a realtor or a prospective client, I would add their name and email address to a list I used for sending out a monthly newsletter I created. The newsletter featured the latest news from the mortgage industry as well as a variety of topics I thought people would find interesting. I made sure to add the husband's and wife's email address to my list because, as fate would have it, my next monthly newsletter was going out later that same afternoon.

The following morning, I had a phone notification that the wife had replied via email to the newsletter I had sent the day before. Only the first few words of her email were viewable, and they read, "Thanks so much. . . ," and I assumed the rest of the email was going to be as complimentary and kind.

Just then, something gripped me internally, and I noticed a very strong repulsion to the idea of my reading the rest of the message. I was baffled by my response. Why did a part of myself not want me to read the rest of the email, especially when I had every reason to believe it would be positive and favorably disposed?

I endured this strange and unfamiliar tension for hours, finally making myself read the email in its entirety later that day around noon. It read, "Thanks so much for lunch and sharing really cool stories about you and your family. We really enjoyed it."

After I finished the email, I playfully derided myself, "See, that wasn't so bad, was it?"

This whole episode perplexed me. I didn't know why I felt such a strong resistance to reading the kind words of another person. Thankfully, I had a previously scheduled appointment with Dee in just four days, and I planned to process my bizarre experience with her then.

My appointment with Dee was on Tuesday, July 8, 2014, and I still have my notes from that session. One of the bullet points I had written down to discuss with her was: "I'm growing aware of how unsettled I am/become when valued by others."

I told Dee about my lunch with the couple, the email I had gotten from the wife, and my strange response to it. As Dee and I were unpacking my reaction to the email, she asked, "What is it within you that makes you feel unworthy of being valued?"

Dee has asked me many profound questions over the years, but this was about as basic as a question can get in a counseling session. Still, something about her question gripped me immediately and entirely.

The moment Dee finished her question, it felt like a muscle deep within me flinched. It wasn't painful at all, but it was very arresting.

I could tell Dee's question had pricked a highly pressured reservoir of emotions that were buried deep inside of me, well beneath where my active awareness stopped. The reservoir was filled with emotions that I hadn't connected to in a very long time, and those emotions were beginning to trickle out from the exact spot where the reservoir had been pricked.

At first, I was able to observe each emotion as it came out of the reservoir, slowly bubbling up to my awareness. But soon, the pressure that was building both within and around the reservoir began to push the buried emotions up to me with greater speed and intensity.

What started as a trickle of feelings had turned into a spurt, the spurt became a stream, the stream became a surge, and the surge became a gush that finally transformed into an absolute blowout.

I closed my eyes and began to sob as emotions flew at me in numbers too great and a speed too fast for me to process. The blowout of emotions soon formed a strong, rising river, and this river I could not direct or control. I gave way and let the current take me where it willed.

Releasing myself into the river's current allowed me to surrender, and surrender allowed me to rest. Resting allowed me to observe what was happening instead of worrying about what this may portend or fearing what I would encounter at the river's end.

What I encountered at the river's end was a vision. In the vision, I saw myself back at Libby's, the same restaurant where I had eaten lunch just five days earlier with the aforementioned husband and wife.

I was at the front of the restaurant, standing in the lobby as one would if their name was on the waitlist and they were waiting to be called and seated. I again sensed God's inescapable presence, and this time he took on the form of the restaurant's maître d'.

God had the outline of a man but lacked any defined human features, such as ears or a nose or fingernails. He was again colored in that warm-yet-brilliant yellow-orange hue, and His countenance beamed with that now familiar yet ever-captivating radiant joy.

God approached me, and as He approached He made a gesture with His arms and head that made me expect to hear Him say, "Right this way, please," but instead, I heard, "Welcome."

When I heard the word "Welcome," everything in and around me stopped. God's bringing that word to mind awakened in me a precious memory I had forgotten long ago, reminding me that welcome was what I had always longed to hear but had not heard, and what I had always longed to feel but had not felt. And now God Himself was welcoming me while looking on me with radiant joy.

Not feeling welcome had produced an ache deep within my soul. It was an ache I was powerless to soothe. My soul had ached so much and for so long that not feeling welcome no longer registered with me as unbearable pain. Not feeling welcome had become part of my core identity, and I had learned to live with it like another would learn to live with a lame foot or a bad back.

I had always sensed deep down inside that something was missing, but I could never fully articulate what that something was. I could not articulate what did not have a name. But God had given it a name, and its name was welcome.

One vision, one gift, one welcome. There would be a second vision and another gift, but this gift would hurt. Whereas God's first gift helped me see that I had longed to feel welcome, His second gift would help me see why I never had.

The second part of the vision also took place in Libby's, but this time I was in the small side room that sat off the main dining area. The little side room was the perfect size for a small family to have a private birthday dinner, for example.

I was now standing in the middle of the side room, and my dad and mom were in the middle of the room with me. God was also there: He was at one end of the small room, observing us from a couple of feet away. He was no longer colored in that warm yellow-orange hue; He had changed, and His form was now like a wispy cloud of black smoke.

A dollhouse was on the floor in the middle of the room. The dollhouse was the same color as a manilla folder and had purple shutters, a purple roof, and purple trim. My dad sat directly in front of the dollhouse, on the floor with one knee up. I sat on Dad's left, which was the west side of the dollhouse; Mom sat on his right, which was its east side.

Dad was completely engrossed in the dollhouse; he could focus on nothing else. It was like he was trying to break a code or solve some sort of puzzle, and he was hyperfocused to the point of breaking into a cold sweat. Dad was acting the way I imagined one would if they were on a bomb squad and were cutting the colored wires, knowing that one wrong move would be ruinous.

I couldn't tell what Dad was doing. My mom sat anxiously and said nothing. She seemed to be watching me while trying to stay focused on my dad at the same time. Mom was doing her best to support my dad while also not wanting to be disconnected from me.

During this part of the vision, I was a child of about nine years old. I was dying to know what Dad was doing and why it was so important, so I tried to get closer to him and the house. But when I moved closer, Dad threw up his left forearm so that the back of his left hand faced-in toward him while his left palm faced-out toward me, like a traffic cop telling a driver to stop and to not proceed.

Dad refused to even look away from the dollhouse, much less speak to me, but it was clear that he was barring me from joining in. I sensed his refusal to let me in was the source of mom's anxiety. I tried to move nearer to him and the house a few times, and Dad's response was always the same.

At this point, God seemed to direct my attention to Himself. As I looked over to Him, I noticed the wall that normally stood at His end of the small room was gone. The former wall was now empty space, and through it, I could now see a rustic and verdant landscape that was too beautiful for words. And I noticed that God had placed Himself directly in between the room at Libby's and that heavenly countryside.

God made me know He was aware that I wanted my dad to welcome me. He made me know He understood that my longing for Dad to welcome me had been the greatest longing of my entire life. He made me know that my desire for my dad to welcome me was good and right, and that, He too, wished my dad would have welcomed me.

But then God made me know it was never going to happen, that Dad was never going to welcome me, and that it would do me no good to stay stuck in the hopes that he ever would. This was why God had taken the form of a wispy cloud of black smoke: He had adorned Himself in black to show solidarity with me as I mourned, to show He was sitting with me in my sadness and was present with me in my loss. He was saying He understood that letting go of my long-held and deep desire to experience intimacy with my dad would be painful and that even facing this decision was hard.

God then directed my attention to the resplendent countryside that lay beyond my dad, where God Himself reigned. I sensed God was inviting me to move on from the dream of my dad welcoming me and, instead, to let His welcome be enough. He made me know that I was welcome to dwell in and be part of His otherworldly kingdom as if it were my own.

I then saw myself walking along that beautiful countryside, and having someone stop me and ask on what basis I was there. I watched as I told them I was there on His authority and that He had invited me. Everyone knew His authority was supreme and that His invitation could not be overturned.

God was inviting me to be with Him, but I knew He would not force me. Because the choice to give up on Dad's welcome was painful, it was a choice only I could make.

But if I were willing to stop waiting for my dad to welcome me, I could receive God's eternal welcome. If I were willing to surrender my life-long dream of Dad being my shepherd and guide, God would become both for me. I knew I had the opportunity to let go of that which would never be and to be embraced by that which will never end.

At that, the vision ended. As I sat on Dee's couch, I was filled with both peace and great wonder. As I recounted my experience to her, she smiled gently while looking at me with kindness and warmth. When I finished, Dee said, "Well, I knew something important was happening. I just didn't know what."

I reflected on those majestic visions nonstop for a couple of days. I shared the story with Elizabeth and a select few others. Later that week, I decided to share it with my mom as well, since she and Dad had prominent roles in the vision.

I drove to their house on Thursday, July 10, 2014, arriving just after 7 a.m. Mom was sitting at the kitchen table, and I sat down to join her. My dad happened to be sitting at the table as well, but he was ninety years old and almost completely deaf. I was there strictly to tell my mom, who could hear just fine despite being eighty-one.

I told Mom what I had seen and what God had said. By the time I was finished, she was sobbing and looked guilty and ashamed. Mom tried to speak but couldn't. She took a little more time to gather herself.

Finally, she looked at me and said, "My lips were never going to utter this. What I'm about to tell you was going to die with me."

I was *intrigued*.

"I knew that God had put it in my heart to have another child," she continued. "I wanted you with all my heart, but your dad worried that he was too old and wouldn't be able to provide for you. Your dad didn't believe God wanted me to have you. He knew the days I was ovulating, and on those days, he refused to have sex with me."

She paused before continuing, "Years later when you were a young boy, your dad's brother Dempsey got mad with me one time and yelled, 'God never wanted you to have that baby!' Your Uncle Dempsey was just saying out loud what your dad always felt."

Mom looked at me, desperately scanning my face for any indication of how I was taking the news.

"How does that make you feel?" she asked timidly.

At the moment Mom asked me that question, I honestly felt

amazed and filled with joy and wonder. Mom's words had given me some insight into my enigmatic relationship with my dad.

My dad had always seemed glad to provide for me. He'd play catch with me just about any time I asked, and only death could've kept him from going to my baseball games. And yet, Dad withheld himself from me. He was a severely private man who refused to grant me access to his inner thoughts and feelings.

For example, during my childhood, Mom would occasionally travel on the weekends to see family or friends, and when she did, Dad and I would go out to eat. If I didn't talk, then he and I would sit there without a single word being shared between us during the entire meal. He literally would not say one word.

Even as a young child, I knew this was abnormal. I assumed the reason Dad didn't engage me was either that he didn't love me, or because he disapproved of me or was disappointed in me.

My dad's blatant and steadfast refusal to share himself with me was unspeakably painful. It was why I had always felt unwelcome. I would've gladly traded a hot meal or a game of catch for being invited and welcomed to share in his private thoughts and feelings. I would've given anything to have the man I love actively show me how to be one.

Though my mom was utterly convinced that God had given her the desire to have another child, my dad was unmoved. Just as my dad had withheld his body from my mom before I was conceived, so he had withheld his heart and soul from me after I was born. It was his way of showing his resentment toward mom for having forced her faith onto him.

Those were my thoughts and feelings when my mom asked, "How does that make you feel?"

"Mom," I said excitedly, "my Abba Father gave me visions with insights about what was happening before I was even conceived! How amazing!"

Mom looked relieved.

"I've already suffered from Dad choosing not to share himself with me," I continued. "I can't change the past, but I'm grateful to understand it better."

God welcomed me. In welcoming me, He made me know that while it was good and right that I had always wanted to be welcomed by my dad, it was never going to happen. He invited me to let that go and to no longer let that pain and shame define me.

Weeks later, I had my next appointment with Dee. I told her about my conversation with my mom. Dee asked, "Did your mom say how old you were when your Uncle Dempsey said those words about you?"

"I didn't think to ask her. But I will," I replied.

I called my mom right after my session with Dee to see if she remembered how old I was when Uncle Dempsey made those comments.

"Oh, Oscar," Mom said trying to recall, "I guess you were probably around eight or nine years old."

Amazing.

Ironically, the most difficult part of this breathtaking experience was moving forward. I spent the following week trying to replay the vision I had in Dee's office again and again in my mind, afraid that time and distance would chip away at it until it was forgotten.

I admitted this fear to God, and He spoke to me about this too. He made me know that He was just getting started and that His gift to me that day would be the least marvelous gift He ever gave me. The gifts God has for His children are endless, and each one will be better than the last.

PART THREE

GROW

"And you teach me wisdom . . . "

PSALM 51:6B

FIFTEEN

ENCIRCLE CARE GUARD

The first time I read Deuteronomy 32:10 after God had rescued me, I knew it was the perfect summation of what I experienced between August 4, 2012, and summer 2014:

"He found him in a desert land, and in the howling waste of the wilderness; he encircled him, he cared for him, he kept him as the apple of his eye" (Deut. 32:10).

When God found me, I had spent decades in a barren land looking for the acceptable me, and I was hopelessly lost. You would think a hopelessly lost man would be willing to ask for help with directions, but I never even considered it. And even if I was willing to get help from a person, I had no intentions of getting help from God.

I spoke very little with God back then, and for what I believed to be pretty good reasons. I thought there was a good chance that He'd be unwilling to help me. And even if He was willing, I thought He'd only help me after I sat through His scathing and shameful monologue about my sins, which I felt I could do without.

Plus, I was angry at God for the family He gave me, a family I blamed for my feeling unacceptable in the first place. Add it all up, and I thought my life would be no better, and perhaps made even worse, if I asked God to get involved.

Amazingly, my attitude toward God had no bearing on His attitude toward me. Despite my unfounded blame, distrust, anger, and resentments, God noticed I was missing, He was willing to search for me, and He knew where to find me. God entered the wilderness—the word for *wilderness* is the same word found in Genesis 1 describing the earth as "without form and void." God found me, He encircled me, He cared for me, and He kept, or guarded, me as the apple of His eye.

Unbelievable.

I've always loved stories about people with superpowers or special abilities. But the closest I ever came to having a superpower was my ability to reject myself and to think I was unacceptable. Rejecting myself and believing I was unacceptable drove me deep into the wilderness, yet God went deeper still.

God helped me be honest before Him and admit my shame so He could show me mercy while looking upon me with radiant joy. He made me know over and over that His favor was reserved for the real me, for the person I truly was, not for the person I wanted or thought I needed to be.

I've spent six years—and counting—learning how to live as myself and nothing more than myself, and both the wonders and the lessons learned have yet to cease. God has taught me wisdom in this secret heart of mine, and His wisdom about how to live has always included insights into His glorious character upon which His instruction is based. Part Three features some of the wisdom I've learned along the way.

SIXTEEN

GOSPEL HONESTY

The Gospels of Matthew, Mark, Luke, and John show Jesus extending His mercy to a wide variety of people. They were male and female, young and old, rich and poor, Jew and Gentile, married and single, healthy and sick, prostitutes and Pharisees, and tax collectors and fishermen. But the people who experienced His mercy had one thing in common: they were all honest before Him. He was unmerciful to those who refused to be honest and to admit their shame.

There's a story in the Gospel of Mark about a rich young man who runs up to Jesus, kneels before Him, and asks how he can inherit eternal life. Jesus responds by mentioning several of the commandments. The rich young man confidently states that he hasn't murdered, cheated, stolen, or lied and that he's honored his dad and mom. I'll quote Mark 10:21-22 here: **"And Jesus, looking at him, loved him, and said to him, 'You lack one thing: go, sell all that you have and give to the poor, and you will have treasure in heaven; and come, follow me.' Disheartened by the saying, he went away sorrowful, for he had great possessions."**

It's important to note that Jesus' suggestion to the rich young man, that he sell his possessions and give the money to the poor, was based on personally specific needs; it was an invitation addressed to the rich young man directly. Jesus didn't uniformly advise everyone to sell what they owned and donate the money to the poor. In fact, Jesus once rebuked a disciple's criticism of a woman who used an expensive and costly ointment to anoint Jesus' feet instead of selling the ointment and giving the proceeds away. Jesus said to leave the woman alone, remarking that the poor would always be among them while He would one day be gone, pointing to His eventual death, burial, resurrection, and heavenly ascension.

I believe Jesus purposely targeted the rich young man's money and possessions, the one area the rich young man wanted to avoid. Because Jesus "loved him," Jesus blessed the rich young man with the opportunity to be honest and to admit he was afraid to part with his possessions because his possessions obscured his crater and his crater was the epicenter of his shame.

Jesus exposed the rich young man's shame; He didn't create it. Jesus already knew the rich young man felt ashamed, and He asked him to give away that which he used to hide his shame. Jesus wanted the rich young man to be honest and to admit his shame because Jesus wanted to *bear* the rich young man's shame, and Jesus could only bear the shame that the rich young man would admit.

Everyone has a crater, and everyone feels shame. People fear they'll be unloved should others know about their crater, so hiding it becomes paramount. Some people use "secular" means to hide their crater; they try to hide their shame by attaining otherwise good and healthy things like work success, social status, attending certain schools, personal fitness, healthy diets, cars, or homes.

We Christians have used "sacred" means to hide our craters, by co-opting otherwise healthy religious rules and practices in the hopes they can be used to make us look and feel craterless.

The rich young man was so talented that he utilized the secular *and* the sacred to hide his crater: he was young and rich and successful, *and* he kept all the commandments Jesus mentioned.

Jesus volunteered and desired to bear the rich young man's shame. Likewise, Jesus desires to bear your shame and my shame. And just like in the story of the rich young man, He can only bear the shame that you and I are willing to admit.

A dear friend of mine asked me to consider the following question about honesty after he read a draft of *The Secret Heart*: "Is being honest with yourself the same thing as repentance?"

Honesty isn't the same thing as repentance, and there's no guarantee that honesty will produce repentance. But, I've never seen repentance occur *without* honesty, either. Perhaps honesty can best be thought of as "pre-pentance," as it is, at the very least, one of the necessary conditions for repentance to occur.

As the great C.S. Lewis wrote, "We must lay before Him what is in us, not what ought to be in us" (*Letters to Malcolm*, Letter IV). Everyone perceives and/or defines their real self in ways that are partially or entirely opposed to Scripture until God begins to challenge and change those definitions. And we will spend our days wrestling with attitudes and actions that do not properly reflect God or His Word and for which we must repent.

After all, God is righteous. Therefore, we conform to Him. He doesn't conform to us. But God will be faithful to make straight what is crooked within us. You and I just have to keep showing up, keep being honest, and keep offering our real selves to Him.

SEVENTEEN

LIKE CHILDREN

At that time the disciples came to Jesus, saying, 'Who is the greatest in the kingdom of heaven?' And calling to him a child, he put him in the midst of them and said, 'Truly, I say to you, unless you turn and become like children, you will never enter the kingdom of heaven. Whoever humbles himself like this child is the greatest in the kingdom of heaven'" (Matthew 18:1-4).

Before I had children, I heard people talk about how parenthood offered unparalleled lessons on God's love. They'd say, "I know how much I love my child (or children), and I can only imagine how much greater God's love is for me."

This made me excited about the idea of being a parent. Not because of the joys of rearing a child, mind you, but because I couldn't wait to experience how it felt to be like God.

While I think it's true that parenthood gives insights into God's love toward us, I don't think the insights are gained in exactly the way it's described above. I suggest that rather than teaching us how to be like God, parenthood offers us the invitation to remember what it's like to be a child.

I'm using the word *remember* in the same way one would if they asked, "Did you remember to take out the garbage?" Remembering a thing for the express purpose of doing something one has undertaken to do or that is necessary or advisable.

For me, remembering what it's like to be a child means reconnecting with and re-embracing some of the more beautiful aspects of children. Namely their willingness to give and receive love, to play and have fun, and to be honest about their fears, hopes, and needs.

God used our daughter Ellington to remind me what it was like to be a child. Ellington was born after I started on my recovery journey, and this allowed me to appreciate her in ways I was unable to appreciate our boys. This had nothing to do with our boys and everything to do with my increased capacity to appreciate others after I got sober. God used Ellington to encourage my willingness to love and be loved, to let myself play and have fun, and be honest about what I feared, hoped, and needed.

Jesus encouraged His disciples—those who followed Him—to "turn and become like children," and on face value alone it seems to be strange advice. Children are cute but limited. They are optimistic and hopeful but inexperienced. Anything a child can do, most adults can do better. And isn't that the goal: doing better?

Jesus explains *why* He's encouraging His disciples to become like children: so that they could "enter the kingdom of heaven." While that's a great reason in and of itself, the benefits compound to become greater still. Jesus goes on to say those who humble themselves like a child don't *just* enter the kingdom of heaven, they're the *greatest* in the kingdom of heaven.

And I'm left wondering why that is. *Why* are those who humble themselves like a child the greatest in the kingdom of heaven?

It certainly isn't because people are smarter or more skilled as children than they are as adults. Jesus' advice sounds strange because of how modern societies define "greatness." We attribute greatness to the smart and the skilled. And we don't covet or esteem the two areas where a child's ability exceeds the abilities of adults: needing and loving.

This is only my conjecture, but I believe Jesus' advice to become like children is precisely because children intuitively know and admit they have needs and because they long to give and receive love. To be a child in the kingdom is to have an Abba Father who art in heaven. Children who know and admit their needs have those needs met by their Abba Father. Children welcome love from their Abba Father, and they happily express their love to Him in return. Children in the kingdom are great because their Abba Father is the greatest.

Turn and become like children. Admit your longing to be loved and enjoy the love of your Abba Father. Admit your fears and hopes and enjoy His comfort and encouragement. Those who admit their needs are greatest in the kingdom, for their Abba Father, who is great, will Himself meet their needs.

EIGHTEEN

SHALL LOVE

"For the whole law is fulfilled in one word: 'You shall love your neighbor as yourself'" (Galatians 5:14).

Y ou shall love your neighbor as (you love) yourself. I've added the "you love" in parentheses; it's not stated in the original. The writer considered loving yourself so natural and instinctive that including "you love" was unnecessary.

I believe we are born with an innate and instinctual love of self. Infants cry whenever they have an unmet need, and they don't apologize whether their need arises at noon or midnight. Toddlers are ebullient after successfully taking their first steps, even if it was their hundredth try, in part because they don't compare how long it took them to walk with how long it took the kid down the street. And when little children have a scary dream, they go to their parents' room and crawl into their parents' bed without promising to "get a handle" on having scary dreams moving forward.

But it seems like something happens to us as we age. People begin learning in childhood—and keep learning as adults—to hide their needs, to dilute their joy by comparing themselves with others, and to pre-apologize when asking for help. And as people get better at hiding, comparing, and pre-apologizing for having needs, they get exponentially worse at loving themselves.

Somewhere along my journey, I realized my life was filled with hiding, comparing, and pre-apologizing. Then I began to realize that nearly everyone struggles in these areas. These dual realizations made me start asking the question: *How can I love my neighbor if I'm unable to love myself?*

The word *shall* can be used to express a command or to express what is mandatory. It can also be used to express what is inevitable or seems likely to happen in the future. Jesus specifically called loving your neighbor as yourself a commandment (Mark 12:31). I'd like to suggest that "you shall love your neighbor as (you love) yourself" is also a promise of what is inevitable, for as (you love) yourself, you *shall* love your neighbor.

My lessons in self-love began the moment God encircled me. I had completely forgotten how to love myself, and I only remembered I had forgotten it because I started noticing the differences between how God cared for me and how I cared for myself. There was a great divide between how I treated myself and how God treated me: I noticed I called myself disparaging names, but He never spoke that way to me. I despised myself, but He kept me as the apple of His eye.

God was showing me how to love, not *indulge*, myself. God didn't pretend I was perfect; He convicted me of my sin and shortcomings regularly and as needed. But His focused attention on my sinful nature featured such radiant joy that it made His rebuke feel like the kindest and most generous act I'd ever experienced.

I became utterly amazed by God's deep and sincere love for the real me. I had previously believed that the real me was unacceptable, yet His Son Jesus laid down His life for the real, imperfect me. As I spent time with Him, I felt Him charge me with the same words He charged Peter in Acts 10:15, "What God has made clean, do not call common." Through Jesus, God had made me clean, and I was no longer to call, consider, nor treat myself as "common."

The way God loved me made refusing to love myself seem utterly ridiculous. The way He looked at me changed the way I looked at myself. Crucially, I learned that the way I treated myself impacted the way I treated others. The days I was harsh and critical of myself became nights I was harsh and critical of Elizabeth, Tennyson, Asher, and Ellington. Feeling ashamed of myself turned into feeling ashamed of everything connected to me, neighbors included. And just recently I realized that when I choose to live in a manner deserving reproach, I project that reproach into the eyes of everyone around me, whether those around me feel it or not.

But getting better at loving myself made me better at loving my neighbor. Accepting my own needs made me more accepting of the needs of others. Being gracious and kind with myself naturally and automatically grew my ability to be kinder and more gracious with my coworkers and neighbors.

My therapist Dee Parlato has often said, "You have to have a self before you can lay it down for someone else," and this makes perfect sense. I need money in *my* bank account before I can pay *your* bill; I must first learn to speak Spanish myself before I can translate it for someone else.

You shall love your neighbor as (you love) yourself, indeed, for as (you love) yourself, you shall love your neighbor.

NINETEEN

COLD WATER

Back during my time as a youth minister, I would routinely sit in my office and study the Bible. On one occasion, I read, **"And whoever gives one of these little ones even a cup of cold water because he is a disciple, truly, I say to you, he will by no means lose his reward" (Matthew 10:42)**.

This verse shined a light on my selfishness. It revealed how much I thought about my own needs and how little I thought about the needs of others. I felt guilty and I wanted absolution, so I ran through my mental list of contacts and picked someone at random to give cold water.

I hate to admit this, but I was using the giving out of cold water as a way to make *me* feel better. I cared more about keeping my "reward" than I did about the needs of others, and I'd just as soon have given a cup of cold water to a plant or a pet as to a person.

Ironically, I was trying to give cold water to others when *I* was dying of thirst. I didn't feel or admit I was thirsty, and I'd yet to taste the cold water for myself.

More than a decade after my stint as a professional Christian, God met me and invited me to be myself. As I settled into myself, I noticed and felt how thirsty I was. I admitted my thirst to God, and He gave me a drink of indescribably delicious and cold water while looking at me with radiant joy. I now routinely admit my thirst to God, and I've noticed that when I'm honest about *my* thirst with others, they feel freer to admit *their* thirst as well.

A few years ago, I learned why giving someone a cup of cold water is so rewarding. My mortgage office is located downtown, and I'm routinely asked by homeless men and women for money. I've heard every rehearsed speech imaginable during my years working downtown, but every single person has assured me that they're telling the truth, that they haven't been drinking, and that they'll use the money to get a bus ticket, or food, or shelter.

One day a gentleman I'd not previously met approached me and asked for money. I told the man I was willing to give him a couple of bucks, but only if he was willing to be honest about how he'd spend the money I gave him. I told the man I wouldn't judge his response and that the only way I'd rescind the offer was if he refused to be honest with me.

Shame began to wash over the man's body. I recognized the sorrowful look on his face. I understood all too well how it felt to choke back the tears then forming in his eyes, and I knew first-hand how hard it would be to say whatever it was he was about to say.

"I'm going to buy beer with it, sir," he said while hanging his head in shameful resignation.

The honesty of the homeless man standing before me transformed a random patch of sidewalk on Marion Street in Columbia,

South Carolina, into what felt like holy ground. God used the homeless man's honesty to invite me to remember.

God invited me to remember the many occasions I stood before Him and others looking then, the way the man did now: ashamed, with sorrow on my face and tears in my eyes. I remembered how being honest and admitting my shame felt akin to regurgitating razor blades, with each shame-laced word I uttered slicing me open as it made its way from deep inside of me out to others.

But I also remembered, all too well, what happened when I was willing to be honest and admit my shame. I remembered, all too well, what I felt when God looked upon the real me with radiant joy. And these remembrances caused me to want the homeless man standing before me, the man covered in shame, to feel God's radiant joy.

I wanted that man to experience God's radiant joy with every fiber in my being. I wanted him to know and experience God's radiant joy as passionately and as desperately as I could want it for myself. I wanted that man to experience God's radiant joy as badly as I wanted it for myself because I knew what it was like to be that man. I *was* that man.

The man was black, and I was white. He was ruining his life with alcohol, while I had nearly ruined mine with lust and sexual sin. But where it counted the most, he and I were exactly the same.

I thanked the man for his honesty, and I said I was proud of him for being courageous and strong. Then I blessed him by asking him a question that I had previously been asked and that had blessed me.

"If you could have God do anything for you, what would you want Him to do?"

Our eyes locked, and I waited for his response. "I'd want God to help me stop drinking," he said soberly.

I prayed with the man, then I gave him a few dollars. I told him that alcoholism was distorting how he viewed himself, that it was like looking at himself in a badly cracked mirror. I told him that looking at himself in a badly cracked mirror would always pervert what he saw and that depending on just how badly the mirror was cracked, he would see everything from a deformed and ugly man to a fiendish ghoul.

I said that if he were willing to be sober and honest, he would find that God was slowly repairing the cracks in the mirror. I said he'd begin to see himself better and better and that he'd learn to see himself the way God sees him.

This exchange between two men can be described in many ways, but I describe it as my giving a cup of cold water to a man who had admitted his thirst. Giving this man a drink of cold water was rewarding, because it recalled to mind the many occasions when Jesus had faithfully given cold water to *me*, letting me experience His glorious and radiant joy all over again.

It's like visiting a friend in the hospital who has just given birth and being flooded with the sights, sounds, and love you experienced at the birth of your child or children. You see the friend's newborn child, and you remember seeing *your* child. You remember wanting your child to be healthy and happy more than you wanted anything else in the world. And now that desire, still present within you, expands to unite with a fresh desire that your friend's newborn child will be healthy and happy. At that moment, you're able to wish health and happiness for your friend's child as if the child were your own, and you will by no means lose your reward.

Those who have yet to feel or admit their thirst needn't worry about giving others a cup of cold water. First thirst, then drink. Then pour out from the cold water you have received to those who are honest and thirsty. You will by no means lose your reward, and that reward is to first remember and, through remembering, to experience again the grace of The One who meets all our thirsts.

TWENTY

PRODIGAL BRO

"And he arose and came to his father. But while he was still a long way off, his father saw him and felt compassion, and ran and embraced him and kissed him." . . . *"Now his older son was in the field, and as he came and drew near to the house, he heard music and dancing"* . . . *"And he said to him, 'Your brother has come, and your father has killed the fattened calf, because he has received him back safe and sound.' But he was angry and refused to go in. His father came out and entreated him, but he answered his father"* . . . *"'But when this son of yours came, who has devoured your property with prostitutes, you killed the fattened calf for him!' And he said to him, 'Son, you are always with me, and all that is mine is yours. It was fitting to celebrate and be glad, for this your brother was dead, and is alive; he was lost, and is found'"* (Luke 15:20, 25, 27-29a, 30-32).

I am a prodigal son, and I wouldn't have it any other way. The memories of my shameful and disastrous behaviors, while always with me, are outshined by my memory of when the Father ran to embrace me. I could hardly wait to tell my pastors and my church—the same pastors and church that had witnessed my spectacular downfall—what God had taught me about being honest before Him and how He had looked on me with radiant joy.

I was excited about what God had done for me and in me, and I assumed my pastors would be too.

They were not.

There would be no celebration over what God had done for me. In fact, it felt like my pastors were as disheartened by my encounter with God's grace as I was encouraged and changed by it. It wasn't for lack of understanding that they didn't join in my celebration; it was for lack of trust in me. Perhaps you're either a prodigal son or you're his older brother.

The best part of any prodigal's story is the Father's generous and strong love. It is an otherworldly, overwhelmingly gracious, transformative, and unforgettable love that dignifies all your indignities. If it were possible, a prodigal would limit their story to the part where the Father ran and embraced them, not from shame of their past but residual delight in their Father. The prodigal's focus is on the Father, and they expect your focus to be on the Father as well. Without the Father, their story is not worth telling.

I didn't want or ask my pastors to celebrate *me*, but I certainly expected that they would want to celebrate the fact that God embraces prodigals *like* me. But they weren't celebratory; they were cool and defensive. They listened to my story like a state prosecutor would listen to witness testimony, looking for evidence they could use to strengthen their case while simultaneously weakening mine.

Over breakfast one morning, I told one of my pastors about how God had used the practice of silence to change my life and, in my naïveté, recommended he try it for himself. He listened to me intently and respectfully, and when I finished, he warned me that what I described sounded an awful lot like Roman Catholic mysticism, a label I believe he meant to be damning and condemnatory given we were both Protestants.

I could not believe that this was his chief, if not sole, takeaway. I was in disbelief that one could hear about a Father so marvelous, yet focus on everything but the Father. I think my pastor was genuinely concerned that I not be swept up in what he feared to be a harmful practice. But I also think that he, like the older brother in Jesus' story, was unable to identify with the prodigal. He couldn't relate to having blown it spectacularly, but he was also unable to say, "but while I was still a long way off, my father saw me and felt compassion, and ran and embraced me and kissed me."

Prodigal sons are impossible to miss; just follow the debris. If you're unsure whether you're a prodigal, ask your family. But no matter, there's great news for both prodigals and older brothers alike: the Father doesn't run and embrace based on the damages done but on a person's willingness to be honest and to admit their shame.

All who are willing are welcomed to join the Father's celebration.

TWENTY-ONE

DOUBLE VISION

"Jesus heard that they had cast him out, and having found him he said, 'Do you believe in the Son of Man?' He answered, 'And who is he, sir, that I may believe in him?' Jesus said to him, 'You have seen him, and it is he who is speaking to you.' He said, 'Lord, I believe,' and he worshiped him" (John 9:35-37).

Peace is hard and therefore rare; conflict is easy and therefore everywhere. People long for peace both within and without, but ironically, the conditions necessary for peace with self are often at odds with those necessary for peace with others. The story of the man born blind in John 9 beautifully captures these competing conditions.

Jesus heals a man who had been blind from birth. In Jesus' day, sickness and disease were believed to be punishment for sin, and the community would've attributed the man's blindness to either his or his family's wrongdoing.

The man's miraculous healing became the talk of the town and turned the lives of many upside down. Neighbors argued over the blind man's identity, religious leaders interrogated the man about how Jesus performed the miracle, and he was invited to weigh in on their ongoing debate over Jesus' rumored divinity.

Next, in John 9:21-23, the religious leaders interrogate the man's parents, who confirm that the seeing man is their formerly blind son. The parents then encourage the leaders to direct all future questions to their son since he is "of age." They distance themselves from their healed son because they're afraid that the Jews might put them out of the synagogue.

Finally, the religious leaders call the healed man back for another round of interrogation. He grows frustrated from telling them the truth and the truth not being good enough. He gets bold and questions their motives, so they get mad, revile him, and ultimately kick him out of the synagogue.

A life-changing miracle becomes a living nightmare. It's turned the once-blind man's parents and community against him, and he's utterly alone. He's never worked a day in his life. He only knows how to be blind and beg, and now that he no longer is, he no longer can. His parents were afraid to be associated with him before the community leaders; there's no reason to assume they'd support him now. Seems like everyone liked him better blind.

For the man born blind, the conditions necessary to be at peace with himself—being honest and willing to tell the truth—were the very things that prevented him from having peace with his parents and the religious leaders. Had he lied to the religious leaders and told them what they wanted to hear, he could've avoided external conflict. Had he lied to the religious leaders and told them what they wanted to hear, it's doubtful his parents would've been questioned or felt the need to distance themselves from their son. But lying to the religious leaders and telling them what they wanted to hear would've meant rejecting himself and would've cost him internal peace.

This is the backdrop for one of my favorite moments in all of scripture. Jesus hears that the healed man has been cast out, so He goes and finds him. His parents were embarrassed by him. His community rejected him. But the King of Kings went to and stood with him. The man could only worship, and he used his newfound sight to behold the radiant joy of the Son of Man.

TWENTY-TWO

STRAIT GATE

"Enter by the narrow gate. For the gate is wide and the way is easy that leads to destruction, and those who enter by it are many. For the gate is narrow and the way is hard that leads to life, and those who find it are few" (Matt 7:13-14).

"Because strait is the gate, and narrow is the way which leadeth unto life, and few there be that find it" (Matt. 7:14 KJV).

My middle school had old and decrepit radiator heaters, complete with chipping paint and poor functionality. One day, God brought these radiator heaters to mind, and I realized that I looked at myself the way I used to look at those heaters: undesirable, poorly functioning, ugly, and unfit for inclusion in modern society. After all, if radiator heaters were so great, they'd still be popular today.

As I thought more about myself as a radiator heater, I could see that I had been consumed by a longing to be different. I had strained to reshape my coils trying to become a more modern and beautiful heater, if not an entirely different apparatus. But I was unable to change who or what I was, despite my spirited determination and concentrated efforts.

Next, God brought to mind a majestic estate, like the Biltmore Mansion, whose construction was nearly complete. The outside looked completely finished, and as we went inside, everything looked complete there too. He took me to the Master's bedroom. It was fully and perfectly furnished with walls painted a beautiful castle gray, save for one noticeably unpainted spot on the wall directly across from where I stood. I gasped quietly and wondered how such a small but unsightly error could exist when every other detail was impeccable. I wanted to look away, but I noticed two metal rods coming out from the floor directly below the unpainted spot. One rod was a valve, the other a trap. The rods were waiting to be connected to that for which they were uniquely designed.

My eyes darted back up to the barren section on the wall, and I realized it was intentionally, not erroneously, blank. Whoever painted the rest of the room had taken incredible care to leave that area uncolored. Suddenly, the amorphous region became purposeful design, thanks in part to the metal rods awaiting connection: this space was reserved for a radiator heater; this space was reserved for *me*. I was the last piece and the final part to an otherworldly and glorious whole, and I merely had to accept and embrace who He made me to be.

Thoughts poured in and out of me: what an honor to be included as part of this celestial palace, I can't believe He wants me, I can't believe He planned for me to enjoy and be a part of His masterful creation all along. But what truly blew me away was realizing that the same aspects of myself I had formerly tried to disown were the very features that perfected me for this designed role. Successfully reforming myself into who I wanted or thought I needed to be would have rendered me unfit for inclusion in His otherworldly mansion.

His glory was so compelling and desirable that I would have gladly suffered anything to be near it. I would have gladly let Him repurpose me from an old radiator to a tin can, or a paperweight, or a tacky weather vane on the front lawn. But I needn't be repurposed to have His glory shine on me; I need only be the radiator heater I was, the radiator heater He desired.

The next time I read Matthew 7:13-14, I remembered the radiator lesson. All must choose between the strait and wide gates. I pictured the strait gate, and it was shaped to reflect my silhouette. I had to be myself to enter through it, for it would accommodate no other shape *but* mine. Each person approaching the strait gate finds their uniquely shaped silhouette, and they must be themselves to enter. The way to enter is by being honest, by being the real you, because Jesus died to save and to rescue the real you. Jesus didn't die to save nor to rescue the person you wish you were or want others to *think* you are.

You can never fit through my gate nor I yours. But neither will you and I be able to enter through our *own* gates if we try to be anything other than our real and true selves.

Few enter by the strait gate because few are honest; many enter by the wide gate because many are dishonest. The wide gate lets you be any shape you please and still get through; you may only be yourself if you would enter through the strait gate. The strait gate leads to life, the blessed life, the life that truly satisfies. The wide gate leads to destruction. You must be honest about who you are and be willing to admit what you've done in order to enjoy the life that truly satisfies.

Jesus provides the life that truly satisfies, and Jesus died for the person you truly are in order that you may experience that life.

His favor is reserved for those who are honest and willing to admit their shame, while destruction is assured for those who hide their true selves and their shortcomings.

TWENTY-THREE

THE GREATER WAITER

"Blessed are those servants whom the master finds awake when he comes. Truly, I say to you, he will dress himself for service and have them recline at table, and he will come and serve them" (Luke 12:37).

"But not so with you. Rather, let the greatest among you become as the youngest, and the leader as one who serves. For who is the greater, one who reclines at table or one who serves? Is it not the one who reclines at table? But I am among you as the one who serves" (Luke 22:26-27).

I worked at Ruth's Chris for just under five years, and I was a great waiter. Not exactly rocket science, I know, but I darn-near turned waiting tables into a work of art. Ruth's Chris is a fantastic restaurant, and I met and served many wonderful, wealthy, and successful individuals and families.

I developed a philosophy during my server days. My philosophy was that I'd make more money and have way more fun serving repeat guests than I would random strangers. I enjoyed serving guests who knew me and who I knew were good tippers. I felt I could make as much money serving three tables of guests who specifically requested me as I could serving six tables of strangers.

Ruth's Chris had a monthly gift card drawing, and I used this drawing to help me generate more guest requests. Guests entered the monthly drawing by filling out a card with their name, address, birthdate, and anniversary date, and I would enter the info of the guests I enjoyed and that tipped well onto a spreadsheet I created. With the info on the spreadsheet, I could send guests a thank-you note after I served them and write them again before their birthdays and anniversaries. One year, I mailed out seventy-five Christmas cards to my favorite guests!

No, serving isn't rocket science, but when's the last time *you* got a thank-you note or a card at Christmas from *your* fine dining waiter? I was an exceptionally rare waiter who sent thank-you notes and cards at birthdays and anniversaries, but Jesus is the Greater Waiter whose service is far rarer still.

Jesus' statements in Luke 12:37 and 22:26-27 are truly startling. So startling that I can't remember ever hearing a pastor preach a sermon declaring that God has served, is serving, and will always serve us. So startling that it feels awkward to say aloud that God will serve us. So startling that if one does dare say that out loud, one may instantly feel the need to water down the claims to avoid being accused of blasphemously overstating the importance of humans while understating the importance of God.

Jesus makes the startling and outrageous claim that He is a master turned servant to the servants. In Luke 12:37, we see Him describe a master who makes his servants sit down, while the master exchanges his fine linens for a bistro apron and serves those considered to be unworthy of it. And in Luke 22:26-27, Jesus upends the relationships between greatness and servanthood and says He is among them as one who serves.

In case Jesus' statements don't sound all that incredible to you, let me put it in terms you'll understand:

THE. GOD. OF. THE. UNIVERSE. IS. GOING. TO. SERVE. YOU.

This isn't just *anybody* doing the serving—it's God Almighty. And this isn't just *anybody* getting served—it's you, and it's me.

After seeing God's radiant joy, these statements are unsurprising to me. In fact, they make total sense. How could God be perfect in all His ways *but* in His servanthood? How could He be unparalleled in power yet weak in generosity and compassion? Or unrivaled in His knowledge yet remain unkind? And wouldn't His generous and compassionate kindness be made all the more spectacular and otherworldly if and when it's extended and administered to seemingly unworthy servants whose only qualifications for being served are their honesty and willingness to admit their shame?

Saying that Jesus serves servants, and especially that He's going to serve you and me, feels borderline blasphemous because we lack any comparable context for such kingly behavior. Our modern world measures a person's "greatness" by looking at how much or how little he or she must make their needs subservient to the needs of others. The truly great among us only know being served, not serving. If they *do* serve, then we skeptically assume it's for a photo op or so they can signal their virtue via social media. That's the only paradigm we know.

But Jesus' greatness is of a kind and quality that no man or woman has ever known or can ever attain. His is true greatness, infinite greatness, pure greatness, immeasurable greatness. The truly Great One is going to serve those who are honest and willing to admit their shame. He is going to have you sit down, He is going to put on His servant's apron, and He is going to serve you while looking on you with love and radiant joy. Jesus *is* the Greater Waiter.

PART FOUR

GO

" . . . in the secret heart"

(PSALM 51:6B)

TWENTY-FOUR

THE SECRET HEART

J ust after 7 a.m. one sunny, summer morning, I left my office where I worked as a mortgage loan officer and walked half a block down the street to a nearby bench. The bench sat next to a playground, but I wasn't there to play. I was there in search of clarity, comfort, and confidence.

Desperation drove my search. Life felt dangerous and a bit too wild for my tastes. The world felt big, and I felt small. My singular source of strength was the memory of my otherworldly encounters with God, which I hoped were proof of His future protection and provision. But I was desperate for ways to upgrade my hope to certainty.

As I sat on the bench wrestling with these ideas, I happened to notice a small bird singing from atop a nearby swing set. Later,

I saw a tiny, brown twig, half-in and half-out of the white playground sand, with the visible half sticking straight up toward the sky. That's when I realized how I could use the combination of the bird and twig to gauge God's willingness to hear and help me.

I said aloud, "God, command that bird to grab that twig and put it in the palm of my hand." Then I rested the back of my right hand on the bench, making my right palm an eligible receiver, and I waited.

I began to regret my spontaneous request the moment I shut my mouth. What in the actual hell would I do if the bird in fact flew down from the swing, over to the twig, and up to my hand? Did I think I was St. Francis of Assisi? Or Snow White? On top of that, I had concerns about getting too close to God. Sure, He had shown me He was kind and generous, but He was still supremely powerful and a touch scary. Bottom line: I had made a silly request and felt silly for having made it.

But silly became panic when the bird flew down from the swing and landed next to the twig. My heart screamed, "Ah, yes!" while my head gasped, "Oh, no!"

I sat, frozen, fixated on the bird, anxiously awaiting its next move. Just then, God popped up in the middle of my internal chaos, calmed my panicked soul, and said, "I'm not going to command the bird to put the twig in your hand, because that's not what you really want."

As and after God spoke those twenty-one words, a cascading waterfall of clarity washed over me. As with any waterfall, I couldn't drink it all in. But even the little bit I tasted satisfied me beyond compare.

God spoke with me from a comfortable distance. He was mindful of my ability to receive His words, and He did not want to overwhelm me. God's words were direct yet filled with genuine love and kindness.

God's words revealed that He had rejected my request, but not because of what I had asked for. His rejection was strictly based on my not really wanting what I had asked Him to give me. I got the distinct impression that a bird putting a twig in the palm of my hand had not been too great a thing to have asked. But rather, because a bird putting a twig in the palm of my hand wasn't what I really wanted, *my request to God had not been great enough!* I had merely offered God what was most available to me, and He was waiting for me to offer Him what was real.

When Jesus walked the Earth, He often asked people, "What do you want?" (Matt. 20:21) and "What do you want me to do for you?" (Luke 18:41). When God pointed out what I did *not* want, it had the dual effect of gently confronting me with the question, "What *do* you want?"

But I didn't know what I wanted. I couldn't recall the last time I cared enough about myself to even ask that question, much less know how to find the answer. Yet here was God, caring about my true desires infinitely more than I did and attending to my real needs far better than I could. Here was God, displaying just how deeply He delighted in truth in my inward being, and how He welcomed and invited me to explore every square inch of my secret heart.

As God spoke those twenty-one words, He looked upon me with radiant joy. His joy reminded me yet again that He needed nothing, He lacked nothing, and He was free to give of Himself to all who had need, forever. His interest in my secret heart in general, as well as its contents in particular, was fueled only by benevolent generosity. What God wanted for and from me, He wanted only and always for my good. That I may be blessed. That I may have life, even life to the full.

It was clear that God would never force Himself upon me. But it was also clear that I'd never discover my true desires and real needs without His help. God was happy to help, overjoyed even. But being the supreme gentleman that He was, He would only help me if I really wanted His help. And if I really wanted His help, then I would be willing to ask Him for it.

This realization was both wonderful and hard. It was wonderful because I knew He was trustworthy and true. But it was also hard because the God with whom I was communicating bore no resemblance to the god I had learned about from my father. I now knew that what I truly wanted and really needed was for God to help me face and feel the heartache I suffered at the hands of my dad.

• • •

My dad, Oscar G. Haselden, Sr., was born in a small, country town in South Carolina in 1924. He survived the Great Depression and an alcoholic father who chased his liquor with violence. My grandfather died decades before my birth, but I would sometimes hear Dad talk about his childhood, albeit reluctantly. When my grandfather drank, Dad wanted to be unseen. My grandfather's inebriated attention was nothing to be desired, and Dad learned to hide as if his life depended on it. But hard cases make bad law, and Dad unfortunately chose to remain in hiding long after the danger of his drunken father had passed.

I wasn't around to see Dad in his prime, but it seems he had the makings of a genuinely good and wonderful man. Dad was very handsome, wicked smart, and uncommonly witty. He was humble, preferring anonymity to any spotlight. He was generous, especially to his church, and he fiercely opposed even being recognized, much less lauded, for his generosity.

Dad volunteered his time and abilities. He delivered sandwiches to the homeless at the Oliver Gospel Mission every week for nearly two decades; and he helped people with low-to-moderate incomes, disabilities, or who spoke limited English complete and file their federal tax returns.

He was a man of unflinching integrity. He remained faithful to my mom for more than sixty-six years. And he was steadfastly committed to *never* speaking ill of others while *always* speaking ill of himself.

That's how others viewed my dad. It was nothing like the way Dad viewed himself.

Dad viewed himself as vile and wretched, unfit for man's love or God's grace. What began as self-reproach in Dad's childhood, courtesy of his abusive father and growing up poor, had ripened into withering self-hatred by the time I came around.

I loved my dad—or at least I wanted to—but Dad refused to be loved. He also refused to let himself be known, no matter who wanted to know him or how badly they wanted it. Dad wanted people to believe that he kept them at arm's length for *their* good, but nothing about his distance felt good to me.

Dad cut himself off from others by giving away his voice, a voice that I considered to be preeminent. Dad literally refused to talk unless he absolutely had to, and even then, he'd act as though using his voice and expressing himself through spoken words might kill him.

Dad gave away his voice because words are ways by which we are known, and he wanted above all to remain unknown. Without his words, those who loved my dad were forced to reminisce about the wonderful and witty things he once said and left to dream of the words he might have said had his life and theirs been different.

It was hard to watch dad slink deeper within himself. He became increasingly withdrawn and seemed to wish he could disappear completely.

I wasn't ready to lose him, and I'd beg him to not give up. I'd plead with dad to try to have hope and to believe that he was valued and worthy of love. But Dad was resolved to become a non-person, someone so unremarkable that it's like they don't even exist. Dad was resolved to be ignored and forgotten, and his resolve was too much for my pleas to overcome.

When I asked Dad why he had to become a non-person, he'd explain how he had rejected God by obeying the rules of his church cult and that being a non-person was God's judgment on him. When I'd push back saying this couldn't be true, Dad would use God's own words to silence mine and support his self-hatred. He would regurgitate the Bible verses that described God's wrath poured out on man's sin and pin that damnation onto himself.

That God wanted my dad to become a non-person was, of course, untrue, but Dad invited whosoever would believe it. By the time I finally gave up on my dad, I was unsure what was true. But Dad's example was enough to convince me that my life would be far better off without God in it.

• • •

The man sitting on the bench by the playground on that sunny, summer morning had spent nearly all his years convinced his life was far better off without God in it. But after experiencing powerful moments with God, the man was beginning to believe that was untrue.

The man was facing and feeling his sadness about his dad having misrepresented God. But even amidst the man's great sadness and sorrow, there was a newfound joy.

The man felt joy from knowing that God's delight was in *receiving* his personhood, not in robbing him of it. He felt joy from knowing that God would always be willing to help the man if the man were willing to ask. And he felt joy from knowing that God was more than able to help when and where needed.

That sunny, summer morning sitting on the bench by the

playground, I learned in new and fresh ways that God delights in truth in the inward being. But at that moment, I still had decades of hiding to address. I'd been trying to keep the contents of my heart a secret from God, even though this was impossible, and from others for as long as I could remember, and I'd nearly destroyed my life as a result.

Sitting on that bench, I was unable to see where the journey of the secret heart ended, but I knew I had to take the journey one step at a time. I was confident that with God's help, this journey was possible. And I was certain the process would always include examining and embracing what was in my secret heart, and then expressing what I found to God and to others.

Learning to trust God with my secret heart remains a daily challenge. Most days, I feel almost as likely to shrink back from the challenge as I am to boldly pursue it, and this despite having tasted the sweet fruits of God's radiant joy.

There have been two principles I've repeatedly learned along the way: First, that the struggle to embrace my secret heart and to offer it to God is the greatest and most rewarding struggle imaginable. And second, that honesty is always hard yet always the key, no matter where I am or how I'm doing.

Do you think my eight years in recovery make it easier for me to admit, or for Elizabeth to hear, that I had a slip and looked at pornography? Or that I still turn inward and become unavailable when I feel anxious about the future or our financial security? In some ways, it feels harder now to admit who I really am and to own the contents of my secret heart than it did back then. I feel that I should be farther along by now.

I'm no nearer to being perfect today than I was on August 4, 2012. But I don't have to be perfect, and neither do you. We must both, however, be honest. How will we experience His delight if we refuse to be truthful in our inward beings? And how will we learn His wisdom if we have disowned our secret hearts?

Being honest and admitting your shame is, and will always be, hard. You are going to feel anxious, and it's probably going to hurt. For many of you, the anxiety of the new and the unknown will be the worst part. But for some of you, the decision to be honest will be far costlier, and there could even be marital, vocational, or legal consequences. But however hard and costly it is being honest and admitting your shame, *not* being honest or admitting it is far harder and costlier.

Choosing to stay disconnected from your secret heart guarantees you'll see all of life through the prism of shame. Your hopes will all be tied to shame avoidance, while your fears will be tied to shame accumulation. There are many reasons why people pursue family, fame, and fortune, but unless and until a person connects with their secret heart, the primary motive is their hope of avoiding or hiding shame. Likewise, there are many reasons why people fear isolation, obscurity, and poverty, but without the secret heart, the primary reason is not wanting to feel increasingly or permanently ashamed.

If and when the pain seems more than you can bear, remember that God is like the man in Matthew 18:12 who has a hundred sheep, yet when one of them has gone astray, He leaves the ninety-nine and goes in search of the one that's missing.

In the same way, God will shine His radiant joy upon you whether one percent or ninety-nine percent of you is honest and unhidden. And regardless of where you currently are and what percent happens to remain, He will always journey with you to seek and find the rest of you that's buried in shame and remains unfree.

Only you can determine what your first or next steps are, and you're going to need God's help. I hope you're willing to **"go into your room and shut the door and pray to your Father who is in secret. And your Father who sees in secret will reward you"** (Matthew 6:6).

TWENTY-FIVE

H.E.A.R.T. LIST INTRO

I n this final section, I want to give you a practical example of how you can begin to explore your secret heart. The goal of this exploration is for you to examine and embrace your true desires and real needs, which will, in turn, let you express who you are to God and others.

If you're willing to do the work of the secret heart, I believe you can expect two blessings. The first blessing is you will know and understand yourself more intimately. The second blessing—and the far superior of the two—is God will use your increased self-understanding to reveal Himself and His Glory in greater and greater ways.

God gave us the secret heart as a way for us to know Him. While God exists outside of time and space, His words and His actions do not merely exist in a vacuum. He has chosen to reveal Himself in the context of real time and real space; He has chosen to reveal Himself in the context of *your* time and *your* space.

The God of the Universe values your true desires and real needs. He delights in truth in the inward being (Psalms 51:6), and the verse doesn't put qualifiers on that delight. The magnificence of this reality cannot be overstated. You don't have to wait until you're "fixed" to offer yourself to God. You don't have to hide until you think God will see more "good" in you than "bad." You need only come to God as you are at present, and He will begin conforming you to the image of His Son right where you stand. And He'll do so while looking upon you with love and showering you with radiant joy.

God values what's presently true of you, and you can be honest with Him, whether it's fear about an upcoming surgery or hope that a child makes their sports team. He'll help you sort out your anger with a sibling and guide you as you ask Him for help with the conversation you want to have with your spouse.

Isn't that amazing? Especially when you consider that God gives to us even though we cannot properly repay His kindness. God loves us because He is love, not because you and I are inherently lovable.

But here's something more amazing still: God values what's in our secret hearts while knowing that He is, in fact, *our deepest, truest desire and our greatest, most real need.*

God, knowing He's our true desire and real need, would be completely justified to dismiss outright anything present in our secret hearts besides Himself. But He doesn't. Instead, God patiently loves and leads until *we know* that He is our true desire and real need.

God knows we can't help but think, "If I can just get 'this' or if God will just do 'that' for me, then my life will be awesome!" But it usually turns out that if and when "this" or "that" happens, we get a brief pleasure hit before our lives just return to normal.

You and I think our lives will be made whole by another person, or a better car, or a different job, or a bigger house, but they won't. While people and cars and jobs and houses can be good things, they cannot completely satisfy our true desires and real needs. Only God can. God will always be our deepest desire and our most real need.

I'm grateful that God, in His humility, meets us where we are and delights in truth in our inward being without putting qualifiers on what those truths currently may be. I'm grateful He knows that all truth leads back to Him eventually. I'm grateful that He meets us where we are, and patiently guides us to the realization that He is what we truly desire and who we really need.

It's time to introduce you to The H.E.A.R.T. list exercise, which I hope will help you better understand yourself and God. If you already have a practice for discovering and embracing the real you, then stick with what works.

TWENTY-SIX

THE H.E.A.R.T. LIST

Monday, April 20, 2020, was as normal a Monday as could be expected during the Coronavirus pandemic. I drove to work, made myself a fresh, hot cup of coffee, and sat down to spend fifteen minutes alone with God in silence. There have been many occasions where I've come to God under duress from unmet needs and paralyzed with fear, but on this day, I was merely doing a self-check-up and check-in.

Being honest and admitting my shame has always been hard. It was hard, especially at first, simply to identify what I was feeling, what I desired, and what I needed. And then once I successfully identified those feelings, desires, and needs, it was hard to express myself to God and others.

Being honest and admitting my shame is *still* hard, and I've learned that if I'm going to do hard things then I'm going to need help. That help has come in the form of a few basic questions. These questions help guide me to examine and prepare me to embrace whatever is in my secret heart.

The questions are:

"What am I feeling?"

"Is there anyone or anything I'm afraid of?"

"Is there anyone or anything I'm resisting or avoiding?"

"Is there anything in my life I wish were different?"

My answers to these questions can, and usually will, vary from day to day, and I use a given day's answers to determine my next steps.

On Monday, April 20, my general questions were immediately met by clear and precise answers, which was very uncommon. On that Monday, for whatever reasons, the answers came up and out of me like candies in a PEZ dispenser.

Unsure how many answers there would ultimately be, I grabbed pen and paper and wrote them down. The list ended up being seven items long, and the items ranged from telling Elizabeth I love her to paying a collection for a check I accidentally bounced from our Health Savings Account in 2018. You can see the original list on the following page:

These items were on and in my heart. They were my heart's list, and they deserved my attention. I intuitively knew how I wanted to respond to a few of the items, while other items would either take more time or would require input or assistance from another person. I took immediate action on three of the items, and afterward, I felt incredible! I felt courageous, real, principled, more whole, more relaxed, more peaceful, and strong.

The H.E.A.R.T. list is like the Ctrl + Alt + Del of the soul (Command + Option + Esc for Mac users). Pressing Ctrl + Alt + Del on your computer opens up a task manager from which you can see what programs and processes are running. The task manager lets you see how much of your memory and resources are being tied up by various programs and processes and, crucially, it's how you can learn whether you have any programs running in the background. Even if you're unaware of any background programs, the programs still use up portions of your present and available resources.

For example, the bounced HSA check had plagued me for two years by the time it made it onto my H.E.A.R.T. list. I felt pangs of shame each time I went into my bank and my pharmacy, or when I saw the returned check sitting on the back corner of my desk at work. I may have only thought about it once a month, but it still occupied a portion of my attention and emotional energy. It was like having a program open on my computer that intermittently pops up to remind me it needs my attention.

After I added the bounced HSA check to my H.E.A.R.T. list, I decided to pay the collection agency that held the debt. I found the last collection notice I had received and went to the website. I entered the agency's account number and learned that my collection had been sold to a different agency. I searched online for the new debt collection agency, found it, and went to *their* website. But I was unable to find my account. I searched the site for a contact number, found one, and called it, but I had to leave a voicemail. I waited, hoping they would call me back.

My phone rang a couple of hours later. Someone with a number my phone did not recognize was calling, and I answered. I spoke with a very nice lady who located my account and took my payment. After we hung up she emailed me a paid receipt, and I threw my fists in the air like I ruled the world. I triumphantly pulled up my internal "program" for the bounced check that had both irritated and haunted me for two years and closed it for good.

The H.E.A.R.T. list exercise gave me a way to improve my life exponentially. I was freed from anticipating the unexpected pangs of shame related to the bounced check. And space and resources that had been used to keep that program open were now freed up and could be used to help me improve performance in other areas.

The increased bandwidth and resources allowed me to be more

fully present wherever I was and with whatever I was doing. The H.E.A.R.T. list exercise didn't *create* that bounced check item; it allowed me to become aware of the item and understand that it deserved my attention.

Some people already know how to listen to their hearts and to figure out what actions they'd like to take in response. But there are also loads of people who don't know their heart at all. You must be connected to your secret heart before you can make a H.E.A.R.T. list. If you're unsure of how to reconnect to your secret heart, the H.E.A.R.T acronym may be helpful:

H – onor
E – mbrace
A – ction
R – epeat
T – hrive!

HONOR

Honoring your heart is the crucial first step and sets the tone for the entire experience. You honor your heart by regarding it with admiration, respect, and warm approval. This may feel awkward and even uncomfortable at first, but don't give up! You are giving your heart the undivided attention it has craved for a long time, and you'll be rewarded for it. I like to let my heart know how much I appreciate it and that I want to hear what it has to say.

Another reason why I chose the word *honor* for this part of the exercise is because of how we use the word to describe the fulfilling of an obligation or the keeping of an agreement. You're going to be reminded of things you said you'd do but haven't, and things you said you wouldn't do but have. This is an opportunity to live up to or fulfill the commitments you've made, or else to admit to yourself and others that you have not, cannot, or will not fulfill them.

EMBRACE

I *tell* my heart I appreciate it by honoring it; I *show* my heart I appreciate it by embracing what's in it. Embracing your heart means having a happy and ready acceptance of who it is and what it wants to show you. Remember, during this stage of the process, you're going to be reintroduced to many items you have abandoned or ignored for years, if not decades. As long as these items remain disowned, you must omit them from the story you're telling others, which means you're not offering others the real you. You can't offer others the real you until you embrace these desires, feelings, and needs.

Embracing the desires, feelings, and needs that you find in your secret heart works to gather these formerly disowned items and let's you reintegrate them within the whole. Refusing to honor and embrace the items in your secret heart doesn't make the items go away, it just turns them into stranded stragglers. These stranded stragglers suck up a portion of your attention and emotional energy, and the attention and energy diverted to them will remain unavailable for further use until they are owned and embraced.

ACTION

When you honor and embrace your secret heart, you'll start to intuitively know the actions you want or need to take in response. And let me be clear: you aren't making a list of items for someone else to do! This is a list of actions that, if taken, would properly and practically honor yourself and your heart. In other words, you can't make someone respect you, but you can express that their disrespect hurts and that you hope they'll be more respectful of you in the future.

These will be the most vigorous, exciting, and meaningful actions of your life! And do you know why? Because the actions that honor your secret heart are inherently real and they always produce real stakes.

Whether the action is sharing the gospel with someone, confronting someone about their vice or admitting your own, asking the girl to coffee, applying for that job, or writing that book, the stakes will be quite real. Sometimes you'll win, and sometimes you'll lose. But either way, you'll be able to say that your "place shall never be with those cold and timid souls who neither know victory or defeat."*

REPEAT

Spend time with God in silence and ask for His help again, and again, and again. Even when nothing noteworthy happens, it's still time well spent. Showing up in one area repeatedly strengthens your ability to show up in all areas.

THRIVE!

I truly believe the H.E.A.R.T. list is a way to thrive. It allows someone to experience life more deeply and to enjoy life more fully. You're going to notice that you're becoming more fully present and that you're developing a better sense of where you're gifted and what you enjoy doing. These gains converge to yield not just greater success, but success accompanied by feelings of sincere fulfillment.

This doesn't mean the H.E.A.R.T. list process is easy or that all the actions you take will be fun. If you recall, one of the items on my original H.E.A.R.T. list was "Tell E that I love her." You might assume that was easy, and maybe it would be for you. But Elizabeth and I stopped saying "I love you" to each other in 2006 because it was no longer true. I've *felt* love for her many times since then, but

---

* Excerpt from the speech "Citizenship in a Republic" delivered at The Sorbonne Paris, France April 25, 1910.

I probably haven't heard or said "I love you" more than a half dozen times during those fourteen years out of fear that she doesn't feel the same or because it might be a painful reminder of our sordid past.

Also, you don't have to be perfect to thrive. I finally told Elizabeth I loved her months after I made my H.E.A.R.T. list, and it was hard to summon the courage to tell her even then. She didn't tell me she loved me back, and that was okay. My H.E.A.R.T. list is about the actions I want to take; it will *never* involve actions I feel others should take.

Living life as yourself and nothing but yourself requires you to be courageous and brave. It's a narrow way that few find *because* of the courage and bravery that's required.

What might your life become if you were to stop hiding and be honest? What do you want? And what do you want Jesus to do for you? I hope you're willing to find out.

The hard and wonderful reality is that God delights in truth in the inward being, regardless of how long you've been on this incredible journey or how far you've made it. Always remember: His favor is reserved for those who are honest before Him and willing to admit their shame.

EPILOGUE

It's a few minutes after 5 a.m. on December 14, 2020, when I realize my alarm has been ringing for a while. I reflexively bolt out of bed and silence the alarm only to notice that my body's vital signs don't jibe with my setting. I'm standing in our lightless bedroom, which save for me is still and silent, but my vitals reflect my having just narrowly avoided some kind of disaster. My pulse is elevated, there's residual adrenaline coursing through my veins, my brain is hyper-aware in some respects but foggy in others, and I'm filled with the kind of nervous, joy-less excitement that's reserved for root canals or cancer screenings.

Although groggy, I'm sufficiently awake to know these bio responses aren't due to my having just narrowly avoided disaster, because I'd been sleeping. Then I remembered that I *had* just narrowly escaped what felt like clear and present danger; it's just that the clear and present danger had been part of a disturbing dream.

My dream took place in the neighborhood where I grew up. In the dream, I'm standing in the front yard of what seems to be my house when I notice two young women on an afternoon walk. I make cordial eye contact with the women, before deciding to lustfully drink in their beauty once their backs are turned to me. I assume they won't notice my lustful stares, but they do; neither of the young women ever turns around or says a word, yet I know for certain that I've violated their boundaries and that my lustful stares have made them very uncomfortable.

My lustful behaviors, as always, leave me remorseful and ashamed, especially once I realize that one of my neighbors had been out in the yard watering her plants and had seen the whole thing. The neighbor is an older woman, seemingly in her seventies, and I can feel her angry gaze and scornful disapproval. I desperately want her to know that I hadn't intended to make the women feel uncomfortable and that I was truly sorry for my actions.

I walk over to my neighbor and stand on my side of the small fence that adjoins our properties. I tell her that I'm a sex addict, and I try to describe the nature of the addiction. I confirm that what I did—objectifying two young women as sex objects—is very common among sex addicts, as if my neighbor learning that my behaviors are in line with expectations might ease her worried mind. I'm hoping she can see that my having made the girls feel uncomfortable had been an honest mistake.

The older woman listens respectfully and intently. She doesn't respond to me with words, but her face, filled with bewilderment and disgust in equal measure, says it all: though my neighbor can only understand a little bit of what I'm saying, she doesn't like even the little bit she understands.

This is the moment in the dream when all becomes clear: I cannot explain away or undo the discomfort I've created in the two young women, and, therefore, the judgment levied against me by my neighbor must remain. I'm just beginning to imagine the possible repercussions for my actions, which fill me with overwhelming dread, when suddenly I'm rescued by my alarm, which I notice has been ringing for a while.

After I reflexively bolt out of bed and silence the alarm, I stand in my dark and still bedroom feeling immense relief after realizing that I'd only misbehaved in my dreams. But my relief is tempered by an uneasy awareness that dreams can, and sometimes do, come true. The dream serves as a sobering reminder that while I may be finished with this book, my life story is still being written.

I'm unspeakably proud of *The Secret Heart*. I'm grateful that God has enabled me to move from hiding to wholeness. I'm grateful He's encouraged me to let you see my selfish choices and moral failures up close and personal and, most especially, His amazing grace.

But what my dream drilled home was that it's not as hard for me to admit my shameful past as it is for me to admit my present weaknesses and future fears. And here's what I hate having to admit: my life, especially my marriage, is filled with painful and unsettling reminders that *I'm not yet completely whole.*

God's grace has enabled me to move more and more of my life out from hiding since the events of August 4, 2012. And I'm undoubtedly much more whole today than I've been at any other point in my life. But I'm still not *completely* whole.

I've grown more whole as I've grown more honest, and both my honesty and my wholeness have grown gradually over time. But the various parts of my life haven't grown more whole in lockstep, and some will remain unwhole and unhealed until the day I die.

God's kindness has healed many, but not all, of my wounds. God's kindness has healed many, but not all, of the wounds Elizabeth has suffered during our almost twenty years of marriage. It's not uncommon for her and me to question, both quietly to ourselves and sometimes aloud to each other, whether our marriage can survive the damages done. While I fully expect that

Elizabeth and I will still be married a decade from now, I cannot guarantee it.

Admitting I can't guarantee I'll still be married to Elizabeth in a decade is both hard and scary. Hard and scary enough that I typed, then erased, then re-typed the sentence numerous times. I *want* to end the book without including that sentence; I want you and I to assume that my life and my marriage ends happily ever after.

But if I omitted that sentence, I'd be omitting it based on my cowardice and not based on God's promises to me. God has not promised to cancel all the consequences of my choices nor to immediately heal everything in my life, including my marriage. Nor does He promise to exempt you from the painful consequences of your past choices or to immediately heal everything in your life if only you'll stop hiding and start experiencing His delight in truth in your inward being.

I've been married to Elizabeth for almost twenty years, yet I've only been a husband to her for eight. Only in the last five years have we enjoyed enough social and economic stability to relate to each other without having a crisis blaring in the background, and even during those five years, I've found new ways to complicate our marriage.

I often worry there might be too much water under the bridge for us to thrive. I'm often fearful that past hurts might prevent us from sharing the intimacy we both long to experience. Elizabeth still has a hard time resting in the belief that I'll love, protect, and serve her when our past has conditioned her to stay on guard in case I find new and increasingly painful ways to betray her trust and said belief.

It's hard for Elizabeth to trust my personal growth, and I get it. I feel sad and guilty for asking her to trust me today when I've been so untrustworthy in the past. And yet, I'm no longer the man

I was, and I often feel discouraged when, despite my growth, I'm viewed that way. And feelings of discouragement are often accompanied by taunting visions where the prize of sustained marital intimacy will always remain just beyond my reach.

There's an old adage in the recovery community that a person should give God the same amount of time to restore their life as they took to ruin it, and by that logic, I'm still less than halfway along restoration's road. But that adage, even if assumed to be true, only speaks to restoration's *when*; it makes no promises about *what* may be restored. In other words, you should be prepared to move from hiding to wholeness without the safety of guarantees regarding what will be made whole and how that wholeness will occur.

Perhaps I'm writing this epilogue as a way to remind myself that while God is indeed making all things new, He will do it in His own way and according to His own time. Perhaps I'm writing this epilogue as a way to admit I'm powerless to control the present and the future.

But I choose to end this epilogue and, therefore, *The Secret Heart*, with a few things that I *can* guarantee:

That God will delight in truth in your inward being.

That you'll enjoy increasing wholeness *as* you move more and more out of hiding.

That moving out from hiding and into wholeness will be painful, but also that moving out from hiding and into wholeness will put a newfound joy in your heart.

That with God all things are possible, and yet the probability is incredibly low that everything in your life and all your relationships will be instantly made whole. That's especially true for your marriage. Or at least that's been especially true for mine.

And finally, that the process moving forward will be the same however God chooses to bring healing and wholeness to your life and your relationships: by your deciding daily to be honest before

God, to be willing to admit your shame, to believe you'll enjoy His delight in truth in your inward being, and that He'll teach you wisdom in your secret heart.